THE MEDICAL
SCHOOL INTERVIEW

THE MEDICAL SCHOOL INTERVIEW: SECRETS AND A SYSTEM FOR SUCCESS

Jeremiah Fleenor, MD, MBA

shift 4 Publishing, LLC

The Medical School Interview:
Secrets and a System for Success
is written by Jeremiah Fleenor
Copyright © 2006
All rights reserved.

Published and Printed by:
shift 4 Publishing, LLC
P.O. Box 18916
Denver, CO 80218
www.shift4publishing.com

Printed in the United States of America

I.S.B.N. 0-977955-90-7

TABLE OF CONTENTS

1. SEEING IT FROM THEIR POINT OF VIEW
-Covering the Costs of Medical Education
-A Mission for State Schools
-The Emotional Factor: Have a Heart
-Protection for the Applicant *(The Story of Brad)*

2. WHAT ADMISSIONS COMMITTEES WANT
-One of Us
-Making the Cut on Paper
-The Personal Statement

3. ESSENTIALS TO CONVEY DURING
THE INTERVIEW
-The "Big 3"
-What is your experience in medicine?
-Do you have the discipline and longevity
   to make it through medical school?
-Have you thought about
   (and to some degree understand)
   the current and future state of medicine?

ABOUT THE AUTHOR

Jeremiah Fleenor, MD, MBA, was a Hospital Corpsman (medic) in the U.S. Navy for 4-1/2 years. He completed the majority of his undergraduate work, medical school and Master of Business Administration at the University of Colorado at Denver and Health Sciences Center (UCDHSC). He is currently a member of the Health Care Careers Committee at the UCDHSC, where he interviews medical school applicants as part of the process for the "committee letter." Dr. Fleenor has been a member for several years. He is in the Emergency Medicine Residency program (class of 2010) at the famed Cook County Hospital in Chicago, Illinois.

DEDICATION

To my Lord-
who has made this and all things possible

ACKNOWLEDGEMENTS

A special thanks goes to all the professors and teachers who have dedicated their lives to educating people in hopes of a better tomorrow, especially Dr. Charles Ferguson.

Thank you to all of the students who pour themselves into becoming physicians and serving others.

A special thanks goes to Diedrich's Coffee "The Garage" for the countless hours in the "office" and the gallons of coffee.

DISCLAIMER

Contained in these pages is information about medical school interviews and techniques that have been personally useful. This book is intended to be utilized in conjunction with all other available material and you are advised to read as broadly as possible on this and associated subjects. Unfortunately, success cannot be guaranteed and results may very. None of the opinions of the author or the publisher constitute expert legal, medical or professional advice. If you need expert advice, seek the services of a competent professional.

Medical schools and admissions committees have varying policies, procedures and requirements, which are not static. They can change without notice. Good effort has been made to provide accurate and current information. However, errors may be present both typographically and in content. Descriptions or accounts of medical schools and their processes are not necessarily designed to be factual but primarily to illustrate concepts. For accurate, current and specific factual data about a particular medical school, please consult appropriate sources.

The order and details of stories and accounts may have been rearranged or slightly altered for ease of communication and the protection and privacy of the parties involved. However, they are all true to the original spirit of the situation and in illustrating the intended point.

If for any reason you do not want to be bound by this disclaimer, you can be fully refunded for the cost of this book by returning it to the publisher with a written explanation.

PREFACE

More than 35,000 students apply to allopathic medical schools each year. Unfortunately, there are significantly fewer seats available than there are applicants. Don't close the book yet! It will help you with your first challenge, getting to the interview. More important, once it is time for the interview, it will help "seal the deal." My goal is to help you fulfill your dream of becoming a physician. I have seen way too many students get crucial interviews, only to fail and, ultimately, be rejected. Let me help to show you the inside secrets of the admissions committee. This book will reveal what committees are seeking. It will help you convince interviewers you will be the best medical student they have ever accepted and the best doctor they have ever graduated!

The subject of this book, the medical school interview, excites me. It is always thrilling to crack a code. These interviews are usually nerve-racking, anxiety provoking events in applicants' lives. In fact, the entire admissions process can be cryptic. To first-timers and veterans alike, it is shrouded in mystery, filled with secret formulas and hidden agendas. There are many necessary steps and hurdles to navigate in the process of gaining acceptance into medical school. The process can be difficult, unfair and painful. One might ask why anyone would even want to become a physician if entrants must endure such hardships. People may have already asked you that exact question, adding a look which says, "You must be crazy." Fortunately I am not one of those people. I think being a doctor is one of the best professions.

Unlike people who say they hate to darken the doors of hospitals, I love hospitals. They are fascinating places where amazing things take place and people's lives are transformed. In addition, medical students are some of the most diverse, interesting people on the planet. One of my greatest pleasures is to talk with students about their personal journeys to medical school. I've met people who had entirely different careers, then decided to go to medical school later in life. Others have wanted to be doctors since they were in kindergarten and haven't quit going to school since. So congratulations on a fantastic career choice. Let me encourage you to keep going on this long, challenging road. It does get easier; it is worth it; and every year is more fun than the previous.

My love of medicine and enthusiasm for the success of potential medical students are two of the main reasons why I am writing this book. Unfortunately, being rejected by admissions committees because of poor interview performance is an all too common theme. It is heartbreaking in light of how hard undergraduates have to work to succeed in school. As students we pour ourselves into studying for the MCAT. Next we must immerse ourselves in the painstaking detail needed to complete applications for medical schools. This is tough stuff and it's emotionally taxing. It is precisely why I want you to succeed in your final and most important step for getting into medical school: the interview!

It would be logical at this point to wonder, "Why does this guy feel comfortable writing on this subject?" It's a good question. I'm not sure there is such a thing as an expert when it comes to this topic. I do, however, have a great deal of experience sitting on both sides of the interview desk (see below for specifics). Close proximity to the application process and the admissions committee put me in a prime position to gather information while remaining objective. In addition, my passion for the subject has led me to do extensive research. I have gathered data from current and former admissions committee members, as well as deans of admissions and deans of medical schools. This book contains some of the freshest, most candid information about admissions committees, what they are looking for and the interviewing process. Below are some of my specific qualifications:

- I am currently a member of the Health Cares Career Committee (HCCC) at the University of Colorado at Denver and Health Sciences Center (UCDHSC). The members of this official body of the University write the "committee letters" for medical school applicants. I have served on this committee for three years. During that time, I have conducted more than 20 interviews.

- I have personally been through the medical school application process.

- I have been through more than six medical school interviews at state and private schools.

- I was accepted to three medical schools during my first application cycle (the assumption being, I must have done something right.)

- I have been through 10 residency interviews.

- I successfully "matched" with my first choice Emergency Medicine residency program at Cook County Hospital in Chicago, Illinois.

- During my MBA course work I received formal training on interviewing techniques, negotiations and the sociology and psychology of interviewing.

The bulk of material in this book comes from four main sources: 1) personal experiences with medical school interviews; 2) my years of experience interviewing medical school applicants; 3) experiences in residency interviews and 4) information gathered during multiple interviews with admissions committee members, deans of admissions committees, medical schools and medical student affairs personnel.

My passion for the subject arose from personal experience preparing for and participating in many medical school interviews. Preparing for my own medical school interviews took approximately 40 hours. Interviewing medical school applicants with the HCCC provided excellent opportunities to see the strengths and weaknesses of other applicants, noting where many shone brightly and others failed miserably. Residency interviews provided "real time" testing of what I had already learned from my own medical school interviews, together with lessons learned while interviewing other medical school applicants.

This book is designed to be very practical and as humorous as possible. I am a student just like you, albeit further along in the process of becoming a physician. You will notice my residency is in Emergency Medicine not Internal Medicine. This means I like to get to the point, get there quickly, do something about it and if at all possible, have fun in the process. In like fashion, I will present this material without much fluff, minimally cerebral and as entertaining as possible.

CHAPTER 1
SEEING IT FROM THEIR
POINT OF VIEW

We are usually most successful in our lives when we stand in the other guy's shoes and see what he sees. Although somewhat counter-intuitive, the time invested in this process does not minimize goals, nor require much additional time, and usually makes things better for both parties. Why bring up point of view? It will give you a better idea of what happens "behind the curtain" of medical school admissions committees. Understanding why they do what they do, you will be able to accomplish your goals less frustrated and mystified.

Perhaps the single greatest hindrance to the applicant in the interview process is lack of information as to how the admissions process works. Specifically, the decision-making process of the admissions committee is little known to outsiders. Interviewers see one applicant after another making the same mistakes. Knowledge is power and you need to know the basics. What follows may seem a bit odd for inclusion in a book about interviewing. However, an understanding of this foundational material will go a long way in preparing you for success.

Covering the Costs of Medical Education

This topic ranks right up there with Russian history and dentistry without anesthesia, so this is brief. Rather than focusing on specifics, what follows describes the payment of medical school education in very broad terms. This will give you a general understanding of a significant constraint faced by medical school administrators.

Medical education is expensive. No one really makes money educating people to become physicians. Budgets for education are usually very tight. The primary sources of money for state schools are federal and state tax dollars, tuition and donations. Citizens pay for this necessary evil because it has rightly been determined by society that we would be worse off without doctors. In a broad context, states determine how much money they will give the state medical schools based on the number of students enrolled. There are many different funding systems in place; however, one model requires state medical schools to annually notify the state of how many students they have enrolled. Based on this number (and many other factors), the state then determines how much money to give the medical school. How does all of this factor into the admissions process?

If a medical student drops out shortly after classes begin, the school is left with a vacancy, reducing its headcount by one. A seemingly easy solution would be to fill the vacant seat with a new student. After all, thousands of rejected students would love to attend. The problem with this approach is that, even one week past the start of classes, so much information has been given that it is nearly impossible for a new entrant to catch up. Policies vary between schools as to how long they will admit waitlisted students once classes have begun. I know of a school that only admits new students within five days of the first day of the academic year. Barring unusual circumstances, if a student drops out after the first week, the seat remains open. When the next "headcount" is sent to the state, it will be one short and the subsequent round of funding will be less. Is the process linked quite as tightly as described? Not likely. Does every school use this system? No. But this model is important because it serves to demonstrate the financial link between the number of students enrolled and funding, whether through tax dollars or tuition.

This financial link is one of several reasons why admissions committees try to admit only the best applicants. They are looking for people who will complete the program, not for those who will create vacancies. Let us make our first attempt to see it from their point of view. Imagine that you are responsible for the very expensive process of educating medical students on an extremely limited budget, needing every penny possible to accomplish the task. Would you want students dropping out, taking potential funds with them? Probably not and neither do the administrators who actually carry out this task.

A Mission for State Schools

Colorado offers excellent quality of life. This state has great mountains for hiking, climbing and mountain biking, as well as opportunities for rafting and other outdoor activities. We have a fine medical school, super hospitals and some of the most competitive residencies in the country. We have a very active population and some of the healthiest people in the U.S. Nevertheless, the people of Colorado still need doctors and health care. So what's the point? There is only one medical school in Colorado. It is a state

3

school, which means the education of medical students is largely subsidized by the taxpayers of Colorado, as discussed above. This also means the medical school has a mandate to produce physicians who want to stay in Colorado and provide health care for the state's citizens. In any state school this mandate compels interviewers to ask about local family members, ties to the state, desire to practice rural medicine and future plans to take up residence. Of course, plenty of students are accepted by state medical schools and leave the state 10 minutes after they graduate, never to return. Nevertheless, the goal is to try and minimize this exodus.

Let us try seeing it from their point of view. Admissions committee members want to maximize their chances of fulfilling a mandate to provide physicians for their state. They know full well that, despite their best efforts, they will lose some percentage of their graduating medical students to other states. One way to help their cause is to increase the number of people who graduate each year. Because the maximum number of seats is limited for a variety of reasons, one way to improve their odds is to admit students who will graduate. It does no good to have five students, who would stay in Colorado as practicing physicians, drop out during the second year of medical school. Not only does the university lose the money allotted for those students but also none can become practicing physicians in any state without finishing medical school. The more students who successfully graduate, the better the odds are of retaining them as practicing doctors in the state.

The Emotional Factor: Have a Heart

As we will discuss later in more detail, admissions committee members are just people. Many committee members are physicians or medical students who know how hard it is to excel in undergraduate programs and get into medical school. They know what it is like to pour heart and soul into a dream, to make it a reality. Therefore, committees want to admit students who are not only qualified academically, but who will fully appreciate the opportunity to become physicians. Successful candidates are driven to fulfill their dreams. I interviewed a former Dean of Admissions of a large state medical school. She said many admissions committee members feel personal loss whenever a seat becomes vacant and cannot be filled. It represents a waste of sorts. It is a deferment and/or possible termination of someone else's dream to become a physician, as they were not chosen in lieu of the person who dropped out.

The take-home message is this: it is bad business when a student drops out of medical school. The dropout takes resources without the potential of giving back health care to taxpayers, not to mention blocking the fulfillment of someone else's dream. Admissions committees are so darn picky about the people they admit because they are trying to minimize negative outcomes. The admissions committee has an even more important mission, which we'll explore in Chapter 2.

Protection for the Applicant

Could this exclusionary system possibly be a benefit to you? Many applicants hate admissions committees and find the criteria for gaining acceptance to medical school overly stringent. It is easy to empathize; it feels like we are show dogs, fully trained to jump through hoops. It is difficult not to feel embittered by the tedious demands of each school: personal statement, application, official transcripts, secondary application, answers to tricky questions, a note from your mother. It feels like the purpose is to keep good people out. There is, however, another side to the story.

Here is the tale of a character we will call Brad. He was a very nice guy with a great sense of humor and a quick wit. Despite all of these attributes, Brad was probably one of those people that should not have been accepted into medical school. There was just too much of a deficit when it came to his ability to make the grade on paper. He started medical school after recently getting married and was excited about this new phase of his life. Unfortunately, Brad struggled in his course work and ended up failing several classes. Such things do happen in medical school and he was held back so that he could repeat his first year. He pressed through the first year of medical school for a second time. Brad often failed tests but was able to pass every class, barely. He was allowed to progress onto the second year of medical school.

During the second year Brad continued to struggle and fail tests. He ended up failing a class and was going to be asked to leave the school. After all, this was his second try and he had struggled so much during his time at the school. His wife, however, was a lawyer. She raised quite a bit of noise over this matter and Brad was allowed to retake his final in the class he failed. He barely (and I mean barely) passed the class and, in turn, the second year of medical school. He was now eligible to take Step 1 of the U.S. Medial Licensure Exam (USMLE: is one of three tests that every person must pass to become a licensed U.S. physician. It is nine hours of multiple choice pain).

Brad studied hard, took the test and failed. He could not progress to the third year of medical school without passing this test. Brad geared up again, studied hard, re-took the test and failed. He repeated this process the maximum number of times. By continuing to fail he, effectively, disqualified himself from further attempts. (Nearly every school has an established limit as to the number of times a student can take the test and graduate.) Disastrous!

What does all of this mean for Brad? First, it is highly unlikely that he can ever retake the test anywhere, so basically he can never become a physician in the U.S. Second, he has spent three years of his life going to medical school, but will never be able to use the training as a doctor. Third, he has incurred a huge amount of debt:

	(very rough figures)
✔ First year medical school:	$25,000
✔ First year medical school (again):	$25,000
✔ Second year medical school:	$25,000
✔ Step 1 USMLE (#1):	$ 450
✔ Step 1 USMLE (#2):	$ 450
✔ Step 1 USMLE (#3):	$ 450
Total:	**$76,350**

Brad now has very real doctor debt without a very real doctor job. Further, this doesn't touch on the personal cost Brad paid in the process. It's a very sad ending for a good guy.

OK, what is the point Mr. Book Writer? One could argue the Admissions Committee failed Brad. He was admitted in spite of consistently failing to make the grade on paper. His ultimate failure to make the cut was not a fluke; it was just a matter of time. That being said, part of admissions committees' stringent scrutiny serves to protect applicants from suffering Brad's fate. So, this rigorous screening process is a genuine attempt to identify the best possible applicants and protect well-intentioned applicants who may very well fail in the end. **Admissions committees**

will reject many people who are smart enough, kind enough and diligent enough to be fantastic doctors. They may even select someone who would not do as good a job as you would!

If this seems unfair, it is. But it happens in an imperfect system, with a limited number of available spaces. As difficult as it is for me to say, this is an accurate reflection of the real process. An awareness of the reality can lessen your frustration with the application process. Do not despair! By following the steps outlined in this book you can bring your best qualities to the table and increase your chances of getting into medical school.

To review, medical education is an expensive proposition. In interest of making sensible investments (among other objectives) admissions committees are looking for applicants they believe will be able to finish medical school. Being able to finish though is not enough. Medical schools want only the applicants they perceive to be the best. In an odd and imperfect way, admissions committees guide and protect applicants in choosing the right career paths.

CHAPTER 2
WHAT ADMISSIONS
COMMITTEES WANT

"Ignore the Man Behind the Curtain."

Sometimes admissions committees seem to come right out of *The Wizard of Oz* ... lots of smoke and flying monkeys. No one can identity *everything* each committee wants in a candidate. There are, however, some variables we can almost assuredly identify. Beyond differences tied to state vs. private schools, this chapter addresses some of the specifics most admissions committees want to see in applications and hear during interviews.

One of Us

The overriding question every admissions committee member is subliminally trying to answer during the course of the interview is, **"Is this person one of us?"** This is not based on race or religion, but on who the core person is. They are asking themselves, "Do I see this individual as a doctor?" It is a general assumption that most people believe doctors behave, act and think a certain way. You will find multiple sources that list the skills and attributes admissions committees are looking for: kindness, compassion, logical thoughts, leadership, ability to communicate, maturity and motivation, to name a few. Many students sit down with a list like this and try to determine which they possess and how they want to present their case to the admissions committee. While most of these suggestions are accurate, I always found them a bit hard to handle. They seemed to be amorphous when viewed in isolation. For example, the ability to communicate is a skill possessed by good doctors as well as good lawyers. However, just because a lawyer can communicate does not mean he can be a good doctor. Accountants are logical and clergy members are compassionate but that does not necessarily mean they would be good doctors.

In other words, these attributes need to be understood from the perspective of a doctor to truly benefit you. I do not know of any better way to study these attributes in action than to mingle with doctors in action. I recommend observing as many doctors as possible and see if you notice a common thread connecting them all. You will certainly see different personalities, different attitudes and different practice styles. But you will also see a common bond of patient first, a level of altruism, ingenuity and curiosity about new medical discoveries. I believe there is a very consistent "doctor persona". Certainly, there are "outliers" that still practice good medicine. Some doctors are bitter, burnt out and jaded. However, barring these small groups, see if you find the common theme. Once understood, it can give you a focal point for interview preparation.

Determining whether an applicant is "one of us" is part of another important mission of the admissions committee. It does not have to do with a particular school or state as much as it has to do with the health care system, in which each member plays an active part. By putting ourselves in the committee members' shoes, we can understand why they care so much whether the applicant is "one of us." By admitting you into medical school, these people offer you an opportunity to become a doctor and hold amazing professional responsibilities.

Think about it: once a medical school admits a candidate, barring some grievous mistake, the candidate will become a doctor! Many medical school entrants may be unaware, but as U.S. trained physicians they will be able to practice medicine almost anywhere in the world. Without sensationalizing this, by granting you access to attend medical school, the committee is endowing you with the opportunity to participate in health care at a very high level. It's a tall order to be a good doctor, and they know it. They also have a vested interest in accepting good people, as they may be under your direct care in the not so distant future.

The concept of time is also very important to understand. Each interviewer has only an application, plus a 15-45 minute snap shot of you. By these means interviewers try to determine whether you are a person who is likely kind, moral, not a liar, not a thief, dependable *and* smart. They would like to know you are capable of handling the very considerable physical, mental and emotional demands placed on every physician. That is a lot to determine over a lifetime, let alone within the 15 minutes of an interview. Remember, interviewers are (subjectively) trying to determine whether one day they would feel comfortable letting you provide care for them or their sick relative. If you have in the back of your mind showing yourself trustworthy of such a noble task, you are already ahead of most applicants and we've just begun. Later we will cover the specifics of the interview process in more detail and how to help convey to the admissions committee that you are "one of them."

Making the Cut on Paper

When I was an EMT at a small hospital in Denver, one of the ER doctors told me, "You have to make the cut on paper" and he was right. He went on to say that candidates must either demonstrate the mental acuity to enter medical school by means of a good GPA or a good MCAT score. Times are harder now; you will need to make the cut in *both* areas. The point of this section is not to go over the specifics of GPAs and MCAT scores. It is, however, designed to reinforce a very important concept: **anyone who wishes to enter an accredited medical school will have to make the cut on paper**. This means demonstrating in tangible ways (grades) the cognitive skills to handle the mental rigors of medical school, as well as the remainder of an extremely demanding career. This concept is in line with our own expectations and those of society; we understand doctors to be intelligent. However, things start to get a little dicey for applicants when they realize just how high the bar is set and how demanding admissions committees can be.

Nothing is more frustrating than to be rejected by a committee – it is a tremendous challenge simply *trying* to get into medical school for the first time. Looking at the GPA and MCAT scores of recent entrants into a "target" medical school can be disheartening, to say the least. There are some very competitive applicants in the mix. Making the cut on paper serves a dual purpose. In addition to determining academic potential, it is used to help prioritize applications. In an attempt to understand why this is, let us look at it from their point of view.

With some variation from school to school, the Dean of Admissions (and/or a small cadre of the admissions committee) reviews all the applications received during the year. We will use a state school in the south-east as an example. For the academic year 2004-5 they received approximately 3,000 applications. This school is on the smaller end of the spectrum. Keep in mind some schools receive close to 9,000 applications per year. Each application includes a personal statement, official transcripts, schools attended, hobbies, research work and committee letters or letters of recommendation. Multiply that times 3,000 and it's a great deal to read.

Factor in the limitations of a 24-hour day and priorities other than reviewing applications. There is only so much one person can read. In addition, there are only so many interview spots each school has time and personnel to accommodate. So what is the point? The Dean of Admissions wears some big shoes. The Dean must try to identify the most qualified students, select those who will be granted interviews and eliminate those who will not – without going blind in the process. One easy and common way to solve this problem is to create cut offs based upon some objective, easily acquired components of applications, namely GPA and MCAT scores. Other criteria can be used: has the applicant published, completed graduate level course work, gained research experience, earned higher grades in certain classes and/or has state affiliation? These benchmarks are not as arbitrary as they may seem. The dean of a large state medical school told me that research has clearly shown that GPA and MCAT scores correlate highly with success in the first two years of medical school and on passing Step 1 of the USMLE.

Please picture before the Dean of Admissions a stack of 3,000 applications. She looks at the first application and if the GPA and MCAT scores are above certain numbers, the application goes in pile Number 1. If those scores are not above the specified numbers, the application goes in pile Number 2. The Dean has now reduced the original pile by x%. Pile Number 1 is likely a much more manageable number of applications on which to focus. Just because an application goes into pile Number 2 does not mean that it will not be reviewed. It does take on a lower priority than the other applications. Please understand that many deans read every word of every application. They, and the members of their admissions committees, are not heartless robots who do not evaluate the other components of applications. This is meant only to convey an understanding of the limitations on resources of time, space and stamina.

Schools must employ various techniques to thin the number of applications that receive primary attention. Using standardized, objective criteria provides a reliable and ethical way to accomplish this difficult task. Ask any medical school applicant with a GPA of less than 2.9 and/or an equally low MCAT score how many interview invitations he/she has received. Few will have had opportunities to interview, let alone enter medical school. All applicants must make the cut on paper!

The Personal Statement

There are entire books that cover the topic of the personal statement. Rather than go into the specifics, let's touch on the concepts presented above as they apply to the personal statement. Once again, we are going to try and see it from their point of view. Picture the Dean of Admissions hunkered down at her desk with a cup of coffee by her side reading application number 325. The special thing about application number 325 is that it's yours.

There are probably a couple of things crossing her mind as she looks at the first page: will this one say the same thing as the previous 324? Will this one be another boring tale about their family physician and how she inspired them to be a doctor? Let us hope the answer to the Dean's questions is no because she does not seem to be excited about the prospect of another drab personal statement. Keep in mind that your family physician being your inspiration is not inherently bad and you will likely include this in your personal statement. The concept to understand is that the reader has likely read hundreds, if not thousands, of similar stories. The key to success is to answer the questions, "How will personal statement 325 be different than the previous 324? How is personal statement 325 going to be entertaining and creative all the while containing the necessary components to convince the reader that you should be in medical school?"

Despite advancing years, people tend to retain many childhood likes and dislikes. People never seem to tire of "story time;" they love to hear stories. As an ER doctor it's one of the best parts of my job. I love when people tell me how their foot got stuck in the tree or how they survived a rollover accident or how the three year old dialed 911 and saved a parent's life. Their stories are great and make up for all of the times I get vomited on. The point of all this is to **tell them your story**. You are an amazing person. You have lived a completely unique and exciting life, so tell them about it. Tell them the fun and creative story of you! It will make your personal statement much easier to write and much easier for the admissions committee to read. That said, it will also serve to improve your chances of getting an interview and being accepted into medical school.

Let us look at an example to illustrate. Assume the applicant's pediatrician was the main inspiration for becoming a doctor.

Personal Statement for Applications 1-324: "When I was a child, my pediatrician inspired me to be a doctor because she was smart, nice and always made me feel better. I vowed to be just like her."

Personal Statement for Application 325: "I remember the first time I went into my pediatrician's office: pure fear. Like most kids, the doctor was the last person I wanted to see. The interesting thing is that over the years I started to like Dr. Green because she was not only smart but able to relate with me and explain things in a way I could understand. She made scary experiences much more tolerable. I later went on rounds with Dr. Green at the hospital and felt my desire to be a doctor increase. I saw how hard she worked and what was required to be a good physician. The exciting thing is that I found these high standards didn't scare me, rather they motivated me to excel in school and become a physician just like her."

Clearly Application 325 was much more fun to read. It also conveyed so much more about the applicant. The statement makes the applicant real; the applicant appears to have an idea of the demands placed on a doctor. The applicant is an individual who realizes medicine is going to take a lot of hard work in the classroom, as well as at the bedside. The Dean has a smile on her face as she reads. More importantly, she feels much more confident about this applicant. She is thinking, "Let's give this one an interview."

Although the process seems almost mechanized, members of admissions committees, from deans down to student-interviewers, are people, not robots. Just as you or I, they enjoy reading lively material. Like us they enjoy good stories about people overcoming obstacles and adversity, and love when the good guy wins. Creativity is a key factor, even in writing factual material. What people do not enjoy reading are statements such as, "I will give 110% if I am accepted," which is used in a majority of personal statements. Don't feel badly if you have used this line. I did too until someone told me there are better ways to communicate genuine desire to work hard and be successful. The criticism stung but I'm glad someone took the time to care.

In summary, admissions committees are looking for genuinely good people, as well as a host of other attributes. However, very few of those attributes are absolutes. The committee is not focusing on a specific list per se, they are evaluating your particular combination of skills, talents, attributes and motives. In reading this book and preparing for your interviews, focus on the common behaviors and personalities of most doctors. Remember the admissions committee is made up of real people just like you.

CHAPTER 3
ESSENTIALS TO CONVEY
DURING THE INTERVIEW

"By hook or by crook..."
This is a key chapter, as it discusses the crux of the interview. The answers to the following "Big 3" questions comprise the fundamentals an applicant must communicate to the admissions committee. It is also the very heart of how an admissions committee evaluates each candidate.

The "Big 3"
In the process of preparing for my own medical school interviews, one of the physicians who advised me had graduated from the University of Colorado medical school more than 15 years earlier, and had sat on the admissions committee. The purpose of our meeting was twofold: first, we discussed the interview process; second, we discussed the particulars of the interview. My major concern was whether the information he had to offer was outdated. Could admissions committees actually be looking for the same things they had 15 years before? He said interviewers must discern certain traits basic to becoming and being a

doctor. He felt those basics had not changed, and we agree. I trusted him and based my entire approach on what he told me. I am very glad I listened to him because I was successful in my interviews – three schools accepted me. These are the exact words he used, "By hook or by crook, you need to convey the following three things during the course of the interview:"

1. What is your experience in medicine?

2. Do you have the discipline and longevity to make it through medical school?

3. Have you thought about (and to some degree understand) the current and future state of medicine?

The following is an explanation of each question, which is the first step in developing your own approach to these questions. In the next chapter I will provide an Inventory Checklist to help you gather the building blocks for your foundation and provide specific details to help you. An example approach for each of the "Big 3" is provided to help you understand more clearly the focus of each question. Also, for each question there is a "lens," which is the Gestalt of what you are trying to convey. Everything said goes through the lens. One last note, each of these questions is unique but they are all interrelated. Let's get started.

What is your experience in medicine?

The core question is really, "Do you know what you are getting yourself into?" It may seem odd but this is a serious issue on more than one level. We discussed in Chapter 1 the issue of dropping out and how that negatively affects the medical school, as well as the story of Brad. The committee is also concerned with success and personal fulfillment after graduation. (Will you be happy in the medical profession?) Many well-intentioned students are more in love with the idea of being physicians than with the realities of practicing day-to-day medicine.

Approach:

Ask yourself the question, "How can I convince these people I have seen the good and bad of medicine and, for some odd reason, still want to be a doctor?"

Here is a list, taken from my own experience, to address this question:

■ Work experiences in the medical field (paid jobs or volunteering)

■ Experiences with high pressure situations

■ Examples of adaptability and dealing with change (Ask yourself, "What if I get into medical school and it's not what I thought it would be? Will I be able to deal with it, or will I just quit?" It is an issue interviewers will probably raise, and will certainly have in the back of their minds.)

■ Ability and willingness to sacrifice (Every applicant needs to convey an understanding of this because many sacrifices lay ahead for those who would become physicians. Most interviewers *are* doctors or medical students and know all about the sacrifices.)

<u>Lens</u>:
> "All of these experiences have given me a very diverse, realistic and well-rounded view of medicine. They have taught me how to be a dynamic person and physician."

Do you have the discipline and longevity to make it through medical school?
This is similar to the first question, but addresses a separate issue. The first question was asking, "Do you know what you are getting yourself into?" and the second question is asking, "How/Why do you think you can make it through this tough program?"

<u>Approach</u>:

- Give examples of your ability to concurrently balance work and studies.

- Demonstrate your experience (or at least knowledge of) with the messy side of medicine. I told them I had dealt with more bed pans and wiped more butts than most mothers.

- Discuss your longevity and strength of desire for this profession (Ask yourself, "How long have I wanted to be a doctor?" "What have I done to further this goal?" "Has my desire grown stronger or weaker?")

- Talk about sacrifices made to work or volunteer in a medical setting. For example, I worked way more night shifts than day shifts just to have a medically oriented job. One woman drove 60 miles every Friday and Saturday night just to volunteer in a busy, urban trauma center.

<u>Lens</u>:
"All of these experiences enable me to go the distance and be successful during AND after medical school." Remember, you are not just trying to "make it in." You are here to become a great career physician.

Have you thought about (and to some degree understand) the current and future state of medicine?

This question is fairly straightforward. Physicians play a large part in the health care system. The key to this question is to be prepared <u>and realistic</u>. It is not wrong to be idealistic but it doesn't serve well to be unrealistic. Some candidates come in and say something like this:

"The first thing I would do is eliminate all insurance companies because they're evil. Then I would float through rounds, leaving love petals as I went. I would see every patient in the city by noon, which is good because I could use the rest of my day to create world peace and free health care for everyone."

While that is a fascinating answer, it's unrealistic. You laugh but you would be surprised at how close some applicants get to this answer!

<u>Approach</u>:
"Resources really are limited. Not everyone can get a CAT scan, even though it could help. It is just that simple. However, I am really concerned about the limits HMO's put on doctors as to what they can and cannot do for their patients. I have seen many people fail to receive care their physicians genuinely felt they needed – and that bothered me."

■ Be prepared with a general solution to the problem. Also offer specific ideas for solving it. (No interviewer expects a student entering medical school to have the solution to the health care crisis. But interviewers do expect you to have some realistic ideas and opinions regarding this and other critical issues).

■ A working knowledge of health care systems in other countries (e.g. Canada, Italy, etc.) would be helpful. It shows you have the initiative to do your homework and provides a basis for comparison.

Lens:
"I believe that the patient always comes first. At the same time I realize that there are choices we can make as physicians to increase efficiency and decrease the monetary burden that health care creates."

The foregoing covers the majority of what you need to convey during each interview. The "Big 3" plus the answer to the question, "Is this person one of us?" represent the heart of what admissions committees evaluate. This material is usually concealed from or unknown to most applicants and will give you an amazing advantage during the interviewing process. The next chapter will delve into the specifics of preparing for success.

CHAPTER 4
INTERVIEW PREPARATION:
STEP-BY-STEP

"Let the Games Begin."
The concept of focused preparation is vital to your success. I cannot stress this enough! Your level of preparation will determine the length and strength of your lifeline in the storm of an interview. Here is where the rubber meets the road – this will comprise the bulk of interview preparation.

Overview
It is entirely possible for an amazing student, who normally "cleans house" with respect to grades, to come to an interview and miserably fail. I have witnessed interview performances completely inconsistent with candidates' classroom performance. Why is this?

Although difficult to admit, some people are too lazy or too casual to put in the necessary work to prepare for interviews. However, there are others who just do not know how or what to prepare. They subsequently go into interviews doomed to fail. Candidates who are too casual subscribe to the "wing it" philosophy, assuming the interview is like a conversation with buddies. If all goes well, the interview can be like a conversation, but it is not going to be like hanging out with you friends at a bar.

Interviewing is generally not an easy skill to acquire, at least not at first. For many, the medical school interview is their first formal interview. The worst thing would be to assume it would be possible to just walk in without preparation and nail the interview. Interviewing is akin to any other activity: practice makes perfect. Do babies walk the first time they try? Doesn't everyone fall off their bike the first time they try to ride? Do people automatically understand organic chemistry (sorry, painful memory)? The answer, of course, is no. We all have to work at these endeavors to become proficient at them. An interview is no different. In fact, in many ways it may be more difficult, as it is filled with subtleties and nuances. Further, the interview process lacks the immediate feedback associated with learning to ride a bike. When you make a mistake while riding your bike, you fall down and hurt yourself. "I'll never try that Evil Knievel jump over the Grand Canyon again," you tell yourself. In an interview, it is possible to do something just as damaging, but the interview continues right along. The interviewers will smile, shake hands, say goodbye, and you will never hear from them again. Without feedback, what is an applicant to do? Just keep reading. Note: similar to riding a bike or throwing a baseball, once you learn how to "do" interviews you will have the basics down and will only need to maintain the skill with some practice.

Laziness is not as much a problem as a lack of understanding about interviews and the necessity to prepare for them. Anyone who is applying to medical school is either finishing or has finished an undergraduate degree, or has possibly even completed a master's degree or Ph.D. (There was a guy in my class who completed his Ph.D. in neurology before starting medical school. I just left him alone in hopes that he would not crush me with his brain or try to do experiments on me.) In any event, each of us, even the lowly non-geniuses, worked very hard for years slugging through organic chemistry, physics and other fun-filled courses, just to be able to apply to medical school. How much money do we spend during this process? How many sacrifices do we make to do our best in preparatory course work? How many times do we sit studying in some coffee shop only to look out the window at a beautiful, sunny day others are enjoying? The answer to all of these questions is likely, A LOT. Why then, would any of us go into the final and most important part of the process unprepared?

Here is a recommendation for every candidate: **view preparation for interviews just like a college class.** Most of us know how important it is to make the grade in Organic Chemistry – it is key preparation for getting into medical school so we work hard to do the absolute best we can. We cannot leave anything to chance, so we prepare and study diligently. It is the same for interview preparation. I am as serious as a heart attack. This preparation is every bit as important as grades in prerequisite courses, GPAs and MCAT scores. Another way to look at it is like a job. Imagine being hired to prepare for medical school interviews. If you perform poorly, you will be fired and forced to eat more of those tasty ramen noodles. That should be sufficient motivation for anyone.

At the risk of sounding like a dad, success, like everything in life, is not free. The price tag is spending thought and time in preparation. Trust me, the benefits FAR outweigh the costs. It is not atypical to prepare for more than

40 hours for medical school interviews. The question to ask is, "Is a week's worth of work preparing for the most important step of fulfilling my dream really that much compared to the four (or more) years I have already put in to achieve this goal?"

Personal Inventory

I have probably never met you, but I already know a couple of things about you: you are totally unique; you have lived a distinct, interesting life. In other words you bring something dynamic and special to the table. Inside each of you may be the solution to a serious problem our world faces today. You are on a quest to discover your talents and how to best apply them. However, it can be tough to dig down and organize your experiences, hopes and thoughts in a useful form. Nevertheless, granting others access to who you are (your past experiences and achievements, vision for the future, ideals and passions) is of the utmost importance for interviewing success.

As you start digging, you need to know what you're looking for. The gold you seek is the experiences from your past that "prove", or substantiate, your personal statement and what you say during the interview. Let me explain because this is a vital concept to understand. Almost anyone can figure out the right things to say. Admissions committees want to know what you're saying is real, not just some words from a book. The number one element I see applicants lacking is substantiation.

Substantiation is the Key.

Let us look at an example of how this might play out. Pretend an interviewer asks the question, "Why will you be a good doctor?"

Answer: "Because I'm someone who is intelligent, full of genuine compassion and I have a desire to keep learning."

Good answer, but if you leave it at that, I'm still not sure if you heard this on last night's episode of ER or if you really mean those things. PROVE IT TO ME.

Answer with Substantiation: "My undergraduate academic work has convinced me that I am cognitively able to succeed as a physician and meet the serious mental challenges required in this field. When I was volunteering in the _____ clinic, I discovered that I have a huge heart for people and it bothers me when they are hurting emotionally, physically or otherwise (maybe tell a short, powerful story to support this). Also, I love to learn. For example, I just enrolled in a Developmental Psychology course because I'm really curious about early childhood development."

OK, now we are talking because I am starting to believe you. This statement is a little bit "word-smithed" but I think you get the idea. The point is you need to prove whatever it is you are trying to tell the interviewer about yourself.

To help the process of discovery, I have devised a series of questions that focus on the "hot spots" and help you develop the building blocks for a solid foundation. Remember, you are looking for the nuggets of gold that pertain to the "Big 3" questions and "Is this person one of us?" we discussed previously.

Inventory Checklist

1. List all of the reasons you want to be a doctor.

2. List all of the characteristics or traits you posses that will make you a good doctor (e.g. good work ethic, compassion, etc.)

3. List all work experience
   a. Broaden the list to include your role in each position.
   b. Include volunteer work, past and present, as well as community service projects in which you have participated.

4. Now list all unique experiences and lessons you have learned during your time working that demonstrate the important characteristics or traits you listed in number 2.

5. List any research you have done. Even if you were just part of an on-going project or your work has never been published, list it anyway.

6. Make a list of all your travels, especially if they have been international.

7. Think of any fun or unique experience during your travels that taught you something and/or substantiate the items listed in numbers 1 and 2.

8. List any committees of which you have been or currently are a part.

9. List all awards you have received.

10. List challenging times or events in your life.
    a. List all of the things you learned from those events.
    b. For example, you may have had a family member get sick (say, with cancer) during undergraduate school requiring you to devote much of your attention to care for them. This, in turn, limited your study time and resulted in poorer grades than you would have liked. Instead of quitting you chose to keep going and finish the class or retook the class, to prove the low grade was not a reflection of your cognitive ability, rather the demands of the situation. You may have learned perseverance, compassion and the ability to relate to patients.

11. List your strengths and weaknesses.
    a. Ask several friends and relatives to list your strengths and weaknesses. (Warning: this may be a little painful but it is worth it).
    b. Compare the lists for an accurate assessment.

12. Write the top three problems in medicine/health care today according to you.
    a. First, prioritize your own list.
    b. Second, ask several doctors to identify the top three problems they feel currently affect medicine/health care.

13. Note where you will be and what you will be doing in 5 years, 10 years and 20 years.

14. List your goals for the future.

15. Write down your "free time" activities, team partic-
ipation and talents.
   a. List any sports you play or teams of which you
   have been a member.
   b. List your hobbies.
   c. What are your unique talents? List them.
   d. List any instruments you play.
   e. List any languages you speak and your level of
   proficiency: fluent, conversational, basic, beginning. (Fluent implies literacy in the language, as
   well as advanced conversational skills.)

Completing Information for the "Big 3"

Once the Inventory Checklist is complete, it should contain a lot of information about you and your life. Now it's
time to use this information to build an organized foundation to approach the "Big 3" questions. (Note: not all of this
information is relevant in addressing the "Big 3".) Later we
will cover the use of the Inventory Checklist material to
address the issues contained in "Is this person one of us"
and "Step 2."

Type each of the "Big 3" questions and place information from the Inventory Checklist under the appropriate question. Once you have completed your responses,
read them over and find the principal theme or direction,
i.e. the lens. It often is outline form. An example might
look like this:

**1. What is your experience in medicine? (Do I know
what I'm getting myself into?)**

   ✔ Worked in doctor's office for 2 years as medical
   assistant

31

✔ Volunteered in a hospital as courier for 1 year
✔ Father was a physician and I made hospital rounds with him for 5 years
✔ Taught science classes at an academic summer camp for advanced middle school students
✔ Took care of a sick relative for 1 year; learned the challenges of being compassionate or learned how compassion came easily for me
✔ Broke my leg as a teenager and experienced first hand the good and bad of health care (give examples from your experience)

Lens: "I have balanced past experiences in both the clinical and academic arenas. These areas combined with my personal experiences in the health care system have made me a diverse, realistic and competent applicant."

Next let's address the question, "Is this person one of us?" Think back to the beginning of Chapter 2 which covered this issue. Please take the remaining information from the Inventory Checklist to answer the question. If you've spent time with doctors, recall the common thread among them – the "doctor persona."

It may help to picture yourself talking to your best friend. Your friend wants to know your answer to the question "Is this person one of us?" What would you say to your friend? How passionate would you be as you explained your reasoning? How would you combine those emotional responses with your experiences and the information from your Inventory Checklist? Remember, do not tell them why you want to be a doctor, tell them why you **are** a doctor. You do not currently have the "MD" after your name, but you do have it in your heart. Use the information to help the interviewer and the admissions committee see the MD inside of you.

It may be a good strategy to prepare your responses to the question "Is this person one of us?" as an outline. An alternative would be to weave your responses into the material you have already prepared for the "Big 3" questions. In other words, you may pepper your responses to the "Big 3" with answers to this question or treat the issue, "Is this person one of us?" as a separate entity, grouping the responses accordingly. It just depends on how you want to address the issue.

Congratulations, you have completed a major step in preparing for medical school interviews. The information contained in the "Big 3" and "Is this person one of us?" is what you are trying to convey during the course of the interview. This is the foundation. Throughout the remainder of the book, when I use the term "foundational information" it refers to the "Big 3" and "Is this person one of us?" The remainder of the book explains how you will take this foundational information and communicate it to the admissions committee during the interview.

CHAPTER 5
THE INTERFACE OF THE INTERVIEW

The Art, the Game and Showmanship

Let us make the transition to the details of the interview. The interviewing process would be much easier if the admissions committee would just ask the Big 3 questions directly and simply. The problem is they do not. In fact, the only one of the Big 3 my interviewers asked in a similar form was question Number 3. This means I have some more explaining to do.

The Interview Process

The chart on the next page is a schematic for understanding the interview process. It is symmetrical and hinges on the interview itself. The arrows indicate the flow of information for two parties. I will explain how this works.

Admissions Committee		The Interview	You	
		Step 3	Step 2	Step 1
→ → → → →	→ → → → →	→ → ← ←	← ← ← ← ←	← ← ← ← ←
Big 3 questions + "Is this person one of us?" = foundational information	Questions they use to address these issues	-The transfer of information -The interface -The art -The game	Answers to the questions they will ask addressing the Big 3 and "Is this person one of us?"	The information you prepared to address the Big 3 and "Is this person one of us?"

Begin with the first box on the left hand side. It represents the core information the admissions committee wants, as we have previously discussed. The next box represents the questions interviewers will ask during the interview to address the issues of the Big 3 and "Is this person one of us?" Keep reading for more of an explanation as to why this component exists.

Skipping over to the far right side of the chart, Step 1 is fairly straightforward. It is just completing your foundational information.

Step 2 represents the answers to the questions that the admissions committee will use to address the underlying principles of the Big 3, as well as the question "Is this person one of us?" For example, the interviewers want to know if you have the longevity to make it through medical school but they do not just ask you this question outright. Instead they may ask you about a challenging time in your life and how you handled the situation. You may be asking why Step 2 is even a part of the process. (The process could be as simple as Steps 1 and 3, but that is just not customary.) By adding Step 2, the admissions committee can conceal the Big 3 questions and the question of "Is this person one of us" from plain sight. They also can start to thin the applicant pool further. You may want to think of this as a "weed out" step. The fact remains, there are more interviews granted than there are available seats in the upcoming class. The committee has to make the difficult choice of who they will grant admission to and who they will not. Step 2 adds another level of complexity and refinement to ensure that the admissions committee picks the best applicants.

Step 3 represents the interview itself, as well as the snap shot the interviewer gets of you. It relates to the subtleties of human communication (voice inflection, body language and appearance), the material you bring and the skill with which you combine all these elements. Step 3 is like handing off a baton. You have the baton (the information) and they want it (Will this person be a good addition to our medical school?). There are better ways to hand off the baton as opposed to less effective ways. The remainder of this chapter is dedicated to explaining Step 3.

Description of the Interview

Step 3 is very important and the most difficult of the three. It is easiest to make errors here, just like the actual exchanging of the baton. Step 3 is the most variable of the three and the area over which the candidate has the least control. The reason you work so hard in Steps 1 and 2 is to be as prepared as possible for Step 3. This will minimize the unpredictability associated with this last step.

Read the following story, then close your eyes and imagine the scene. Pretend you are the interviewer. Remember, many interviewers are doctors or medical students. Although the following story is a dramatization, it contains common occurrences from my own experience.

You have been on call and up all night. It was not the busiest night you have had but it was not slow. There was a new nurse on the 7th floor who insisted on paging you every 45 minutes with inappropriate questions. You had a very difficult time putting in a central line in an elderly patient requiring chemotherapy. You are frustrated and your back hurts because you were hunched over for more than an hour. You hurry to finish your rounds so that you are not late for the day's interviews with the medical school applicants. You really like being on the admissions committee and have done it for four years now. You like to talk to the young students and care a great deal for the University as you are a graduate of the medical school. While you do like this position, it is extra work for which you are not getting paid and it is towards the end of the interviewing season. You have done at least 13 of these interview days already. You are tired and have been up for 30 hours now. You walk into the admissions office, say hello to the secretary and ask for the applications of the students you will be interviewing today. She hands them to you and you quickly pour through the first applicant's personal statement, grades, MCAT scores and letters of recommendation while sucking down a cup of coffee. You call in the applicant, smile and shake her hand. The interview transpires. You thank the applicant, shake her hand and send them back to the waiting room. You close the door to the interview room and turn to fill out the University's standard post-encounter evaluation form. You realize that you have four more interviews to go and that it will have been more than 38 hours before you get to sleep. What happens next?

OK, here are some general questions that I want you to answer from the perspective of the interviewer. Read them and the scenario again, then close your eyes and run it all through your head. Really try to feel what that interviewer would feel like. Put yourself in his shoes. I promise this is worthwhile.

1. What is going to make your job easier as you fill out the evaluation?
2. Was the applicant energetic?
3. Was the interview fun?
4. Was the exchange pleasant?
5. Did she give you anything to work with or are you going to have to pull items from the interview to fill out this evaluation?
6. What was different about this person as compared to the others?

Re-run this scenario through your head answering the questions and imagine what this interviewer would be feeling.

Again, that was a dramatization but not unrealistic. Many people would agree that no one should be interviewing in a sleep-deprived, harried state. As we have discussed, this is not an ideal system. In an imperfect world this happens all the time. This is the time to let go of what "should be." Just be prepared for the situation. Do not worry. What follows will help prepare you to deal with the situation described above and others that are even more challenging. You may not realize how much control you actually have in an interview.

Whether you have an interviewer like the one I just described or one who is well-rested and fresh, they all face the list of questions above. **It is your job as the applicant to make this process as easy for them as possible.** I realize that might seem like a weird concept but it is true. A good way to look at your interviewer is as your personal advocate before the admissions committee. Let me explain a little more about the process.

How Admissions Committees Are Organized

The admissions committee has many members, usually headed up by the Dean of Admissions. Most of the medical schools at which I interviewed did two (sometimes three) interviews, each about 15-45 minutes long. It was often the case that one interviewer was a Ph.D. or MD and the other, a medical student. It was common for only one of the interviewers to have read my application (See Chapter 8, pg. 77).

In my experience, once the interview was over the interviewers would fill out an evaluation of how the interview went. Certain categories of importance to the University received a numerical value. There is usually space for general comments. At the University of Colorado, those who interviewed me would then "present" me and my application to the rest of the admissions committee. There would then be some sort of vote or numerical score assigned to me. This "score" became my final ranking among the applicants for that year. Not all admissions committees are this way but it is common.

With the above understanding, I hope it is easier to see that the interviewer is the one who is selling you to the rest of the admissions committee, so make it an easy sell. You should have all of your answers as concise as possible with easy to remember catch phrases. You want to have yourself nicely packaged and easy to handle. Let me use a personal story to help illustrate this concept.

I was working part-time as a phlebotomist while I was finishing undergraduate school. Like most employees, I had to fill out a self-evaluation form for my annual review. Almost all of my other coworkers hated these self-evaluations and viewed them as a nuisance. For some reason they failed to grasp the concept that these "painful" self-evaluations were the main way in which they got raises and promotions. (This might seem shocking to you but many medical school applicants view the interview in the same light.) However, since I was familiar with the concept of seeing things from the other person's point of view, I approached the self-evaluation much differently. I put myself in my boss' shoes. What would she be thinking? How does she feel about this part of her job? I learned that she had to take our self-evaluations and fill out her own assessment of our performance. Her evaluation was used to justify our raises, promotions or reprimands. It did not take too much effort to realize that this time of year was not her favorite. She did not particularly enjoy having to read all of these self-evaluations. People hated filling them out and gave her little to work with. Further, the meetings with the phlebotomists were grueling. Many would moan and complain. They felt her evaluations were unfair and that they deserved more of a raise. This whole process was really difficult for my boss. Once I saw things from her point of view, my plan became clear and easy.

I took that self-evaluation form and went to town. I put time and effort into completing the evaluation well. I used sufficient detail to fill out each section with all of the previous year's accomplishments. I told her how I was frequently called upon by others to get the hard sticks. I mentioned that patients would complement me on how proficient I was at phlebotomy. I used simple catch phrases that were easy to remember.

Interview time came and my boss went over her evaluation of me. It was based on the form I submitted and what she had learned from talking to others. She said her evaluation of me was largely <u>copied</u> from the self-evaluation I had submitted. She felt she could not say it better so she simply used my words (the exact same words). The interview was quick. I did not moan or complain. I smiled and was energetic. The process came off without a hitch. Despite being part-time, she put me in the highest pay raise category and recommended me for a promotion. It was awesome!

This was a great experience because I basically wrote my own annual review. This opportunity came about because I took the time to understand the process and see things from the other person's perspective. What happened during my annual review can happen for you during your medical school interview. I will show you how to maximize your chances of "writing" your own interview evaluation.

The remainder of this chapter will provide more of an understanding of the process.

Six Subliminal Questions

Think back to the visualization scenario of the interviewer and the foregoing story. Do you see any similarities between the two? I think the annual review process described is very similar to the process of admissions committees. What was used to make my boss' job easier can be used to make your interviewer's job easier. The questions below are the same ones used in the story of our sleep-deprived interviewer. In the next chapter, as you prepare your answers to the Step 2 questions, do so thinking about the interview scenario described earlier.

1. What is going to make your job easier as you fill out the evaluation?

Prepare your responses in such a way as to make it easy for the interviewer to complete the interview evaluation. Here is an example using a simple question: what do you like to do in your free time?

> Answer: "Well, I don't have a lot of free time because I'm always studying and trying to get good grades. I do like to do logic puzzles and to go running if I have the chance."

Notice, this person only partly answered the question. He started off with a negative comment about not having much free time. He gave the impression that he struggled to get good grades. He did manage to say he likes puzzles and running. Neither is the most entertaining of pastimes, but they count. As an interviewer it would be a stretch to see this individual as really confident, happy, or even much fun. What do you think?

> Better Answer (easier for the interviewer): "Free time is a precious commodity so I use it wisely. I am eager to hit the books but I also know how important recuperating is for balance. I enjoy doing those Sudoku number puzzles; they're addictive. I also love to run. I'm not exactly "marathon man" but I have a great time just pounding the streets and exploring the area near my house."

This person has done a great job painting a picture. The second answer conveys the same information as the first, but in a much better way. I don't necessarily know what a "logic puzzle" is but I have heard of those Sudoku number puzzles. The interviewer can see this college guy running in the city, making a loop around the local park and ending his run with a pit stop in the neighborhood coffee shop to work on a Sudoku puzzle. When the interviewer evaluates the second candidate's interview he has a more vivid picture, more color and more he can use. What if an interviewer can't remember exactly what this applicant said during the interview? One method is to think back and try to replay the highlights of the interview. "Marathon man" is more memorable than "I like running." You get the point.

2. Was the applicant energetic?

Regardless of job title or status, most people are overworked and sleep-deprived to some degree. There are plenty of statistics demonstrating how little sleep Americans get and the deleterious effects. The problem is more pronounced in the field of medicine. Knowing this, just assume you will be more rested than your interviewer. Go into the interview prepared to be positive and energetic. It isn't necessary to be a cheerleader, but picture yourself as the more energetic of the two people. This simple thing will go a long way in facilitating the entire interview process.

3. Was the interview fun?

Candidates need not be prepared with magic tricks and face paint. It is, however, important to grasp the concept of making an interview fun. This is accomplished by being prepared, genuine, comfortable, interesting and engaging. Always remain respectful but realize this person interviewing you is just that, a person. Interviewers have parents, spouses, kids and friends. What is fun for you to talk about? What are common joys and hardships you experience in your relationships? They most likely experience similar things. Now you have something in common and can feel comfortable with the real human on the other side of the table.

4. Was the exchange pleasant?

Predetermine that no matter what happens during the interview, you will not bad mouth any other school or person. Focus on the positive. Self-confidence and pride in your achievements are fine, but it is deadly to appear arrogant or full of yourself. No matter what the interviewer says or does – perhaps even intentionally to offend – refrain from being antagonistic or confrontational. The tiniest bit of negativity goes a long way in putting you and those around you in the wrong frame of mind. It's imperative that interviewers are happy and positive when they fill out your evaluation. Create and maintain a positive environment. It will linger up to and after your departure.

5. Did she give you anything to work with or are you going to have to pull items from the interview to fill out this evaluation?

Remember how our interviewer in the scenario was not getting paid? With the exception of the Dean of Admissions, it is unlikely any admissions committee members are compensated for the role. Take this to heart. Why should anyone have to workd to fill out an evaluation of *your* interview? Do the work for them. Give them a lot of easy to remember catch phrases. It is easier to work with material than to generate something on your own. Use this technique to portray yourself in the best light possible. It will make the process fun and easy for the interviewer to complete your evaluation.

6. What was different about this person as compared to the others?

For better or for worse, one of the ways humans learn is by focusing on differences. Do you remember the person at a funeral who was wearing a black outfit or the colored outfit? It will be easier for the interviewer to remember you if you present the things that are unique to you. Do not, however, stand out by being late to or falling asleep during the interview. That is memorable all right, but not in the way you are hoping. Spend time talking to other medical school applicants at your university and find out what they are bringing to the table. Ask your advisor about the skills, talents and past experiences of most applicants.

Try and build a "normal" applicant in your mind and figure out how you are unique in ways that are advantageous to becoming a physician. For example, I had significant experience in the medical field having been in the Navy and working in hospitals throughout my undergraduate course work. I also had traveled extensively. Being fairly unique, I focused on these areas. Another example was a woman in our class who had had her own successful business as an interior designer. She was older, refined and very savvy. She focused on these areas as they were unique to her.

As you proceed through the medical school application process, residency interviews, job interviews and other personal encounters, learn to see yourself as others see you. Keep this in mind and watch your chances for success markedly improve.

CHAPTER 6
A SYSTEM FOR SUCCESS

"Could you repeat the question?"

This chapter addresses the Big 3 questions and the form they may take during interviews. Remember, we are spending time diligently preparing so that we can reduce the level of unpredictability and variability in the actual interview. The actual number of individual questions an interviewer can ask you is high. Do not despair! There are ways to approach the situation. Once you experience multiple interviews you will be able to observe many similarities between them. Each is unique, but there are many similarities, from the format of the session to the interview questions. Despite the spectrum of ways to spin the questions, they all address the foundational information you have developed.

The Technique of Categorization

As mentioned above there is no way to be perfectly prepared for every question. Fortunately, it won't be necessary because almost every question falls into a certain category.

The 15 questions the interviewer asked you on Monday may be completely different from the 15 questions asked by Wednesday's interviewer. Not to worry – all 30 questions fit into categories for which you are prepared. Following the steps we have discussed will prepare you for both interviews and more.

There is a great deal of variability when it comes to creating categories. The following will serve as a guide. Feel free to add or restructure as you see fit. Everyone conceptualizes in his or her own way and we are all shaped by experience. This list is not static; it is dynamic and can change as your interview experience increases.

Often interviewers ask questions in a broad context. They are not necessarily looking for specific answers. Rather, they want to see where you take it. Use the opportunity to cover more of your foundational information. Consider how the question fits into a category for which you are well-prepared. For example, if they asked the question, "Who would you invite to dinner and why?" I realized there was likely no correct answer to this question. They were looking to see where I would take it. So I would put it in one of my categories and cover more of my foundational information. There were times when the interviewer asked me a question that I was a little unprepared for or could not readily fit into one of my categories. In these situations I just put their question into a category that was close and went with it. It always seemed to work out fine. If, for some reason, you completely "miss the boat" by misinterpreting a question and you answer it in a different way than they were intending, they will refocus their question or redirect you.

Here are the specific categories and some thoughts on each. The explanations that follow each category should give you an idea of how you can use them.

1. Personal Abilities and Strengths

This is the category for positive attributes (as distinct from personal values). It is for accomplishments like musical talent, knowledge of a foreign language, as well as skills such as communication, negotiation, analytical ability and the ability to think critically.

2. Personal Accomplishments

The focus in this category is on specific measurable accomplishments, for example: awards, grades, MCAT scores, honor societies and clubs.

3. Personal Values

This is a fairly broad category. As opposed to abilities and strengths, values are abstract – they are thought, attitude or philosophically based. These are the items of character. Without making political or religious statements, this category would be appropriate for spiritual or religious beliefs, or political views (as they define your values). It would include such things as your view on health care, compassion, patience and strong work ethic. (Note: it is best to avoid discussing politics in the interview.)

4. Weaknesses

In this case "weaknesses" refers to attitudes or habits resulting from strengths. For this purpose, YOUR STRENGTHS ARE YOUR WEAKNESSES. We all know people who are very analytical. This strength becomes a weakness when our "super analytical" friend spends 20 minutes in front of the ice cream case at the store "analyzing" which ice cream is best to buy. Meanwhile everybody else goes nuts waiting for the momentous decision. I really think this is the best way to handle the "what are your weaknesses" question. This is not the time to talk about your anger management issues. Remember to put your best foot forward. Everyone has areas in their life they wish were better and are working to improve. <u>An interview is not the place or time to discuss those areas.</u>

5. Free Time Activities

These are things you enjoy doing outside of medicine, for example: sports, exercise, music, time with friends and family and recreational reading. Do not underestimate the power of this material. Admissions committees are very concerned about burnout in people who are just into studying and books. This is also a concern for hospital residents. The balance of pastimes with good grades and test scores demonstrates you are not maxed out by making the cut on paper. Does that make sense? You have enough time and ability left over after "study time" to do other things. At this level it is not enough to just be smart, it is also important to be interesting and multi-dimensional.

6. Handling Challenges, Criticism, Negative Situations, Failures

How do you handle tough times? Remember, it is not a question of if, but when the challenges will hit in medical school. Interviewers want to know how you will respond. Include the concept of balance and recuperation via links with your hobbies. The concept of balance is very important. Do you have pet peeves, small things that upset you? Give some thought to how you handle these minor annoyances. Be prepared to address this issue, rather than allow it to become a pitfall.

7. Sacrifices
No doubt you will already have made sacrifices to get this far. This category is your opportunity to let interviewers know you willingly forego some experiences and/or material rewards in order to achieve important goals.

8. State of Medicine
This category is fairly straightforward. What is currently happening in health care and what will be going on in the future? Talk to older physicians and ask them about the transition from the "old way" to the era of managed care. Ask them the direction they think medicine is headed.

9. Your Uniqueness
These are qualities that make you different from other applicants. This category answers the question, "What do I bring to this medical school and how am I going to make it a better place than when I arrived?"

10. An Overview of You as a Person and Applicant
The questions in this category usually come in the form of icebreakers. I'll cover this category in detail in Chapter 7.

Let us do a little practice session. Here are 10 <u>actual questions</u> asked by admissions committees. Assign each question a category. Afterward we'll discuss the choices. As in the multiple choice tests to which you are accustomed, categories may be used once, multiple times or not at all (sorry, that was a low blow.)

1. Tell me a little bit about yourself.
2. Name a person you would invite to dinner and why.
3. Name three adjectives that best describe you.
4. What do you think about euthanasia?
5. If you were made the czar of health care in the U.S., what would you do?
6. What has been the toughest class in your collegiate career thus far and how did you manage the situation?
7. Pick one symbol or object that best describes you.
8. What do you like to do in your down time?
9. If there were one seat left in the upcoming class and I had to choose between you and the next applicant, why should I choose you?
10. Name one thing you do not like about yourself.

The following are hypothetical choices. Yours may be very different. That is okay, just try to be consistent.

- ✔ Personal Abilities and Strengths: #2, #3, #7
- ✔ Personal Accomplishments:
- ✔ Personal Values: #2, #3, #4, #7
- ✔ Weakness: #10
- ✔ Free Time Activities: #8
- ✔ Handling Challenges, Criticism, Negative Situations, Failures: #6

- ✔ Sacrifices:
- ✔ State of Medicine: #5
- ✔ Your Uniqueness: #9
- ✔ An Overview of You as a Person and Applicant: #1

Some of the questions were a little tricky and some were straight forward, which is how an actual interview goes. An interviewer can throw out a variety of questions, and you can deal with them easily by fitting them into the categories you will have prepared.

Bending the Truth

You are about to start preparing your answers for the above categories. Many candidates want to get into medical school so badly they would say almost anything. It can be very taxing just to get to an actual interview. You are trying to put your best foot forward and sway the admissions committee. It can be incredibly easy to cross the line from best foot forward to old-fashioned lying. Please make sure you do not lie. Most assuredly it will come back to haunt you. Further, the medical profession absolutely demands fidelity and high ethical character. Here are a couple of humorous (or sad) stories from the trenches.

There was an applicant who had spent some time in a foreign country. I think it was Russia or Ukraine. She had learned to speak the local vernacular, but barely at a conversational level. She claimed on her application to be fluent, assuming no interviewer would be fluent in this somewhat rare dialect of Russian. Sure enough, the interviewer started speaking to her <u>in that dialect</u>. To her extreme embarrassment, she could not understand him. A stunned silence filled the room. Unless she could convince the interviewer she'd had a stroke and infarcted the language center of her brain, she was busted.

A fellow applicant on my residency interview trail had a similar experience. He put on his application that he played the guitar. This was true, but he had not played since college, several years back. The interviewer asked him several questions about this part of his application almost trying to get the applicant to brag a little or overstate his musical ability. The interviewer then reached behind the closet door, pulled out a guitar and asked the applicant to play him a song. He was serious. The applicant struggled through a song and the interviewer asked him to play ANOTHER. It is an extreme example, but the point is that people do check the facts on applications. It is enough to be yourself, so do not be tempted to lie or exaggerate.

Before you start preparing your responses there are a couple more concepts we should cover.

To Memorize or Not to Memorize, that is the Question

Try suggesting that people have their responses memorized. One of several things will happen. They will laugh, scoff, say nothing or give you the *look* (the one reserved for alien life forms). Some will have a synapse and realize they are under-prepared. Regardless of physical response, the reactions tend to be strong. Even though having answers memorized may hamper some people, read the following analogy and the explanation.

Bridge vs. Stepping-Stone

Picture yourself standing on one side of a wide, deep river. You are starting on Side A. Look over the river to the other side, Side B. The goal is to get from Side A over to Side B. Imagine Side A is the beginning of an interview.

Side B is where the interviewer wants you to go. The gap represents the question. How you cross the gap is the issue at hand. Visualize two ways to cross the gap – via a bridge or crossing by means of stepping-stones. Here is a simple picture to help you visualize this.

Clearly the bridge is a fixed structure that spans the river. In the context of an interview it is like a memorized script. The advantages of crossing by means of a bridge are structural sturdiness and predictability. The structured script works best when the questions are predictable, because you will have scripted the best possible responses. As we've previously discussed the interview is an unpredictable event. This is the disadvantage of scripted responses. Using the bridge approach mandates fixed beginning and ending points. These are unknown until the interviewer asks specific questions. Further, scripted answers in the form of a "bridge" can sound stiff, unnatural and, well, memorized. There is a genuine credibility issue.

The second way to cross a river is to place many stepping-stones, leading from Side A to Side B. The best way to use stepping-stones is to hop from one stone to the next to get over to Side B. The disadvantages are that stepping-stones are not as sturdy as bridges. In the context of interviewing the stones are small word groups used to convey information. Using word groups as you would stepping-stones requires effort. It is analogous to jumping and hopping, as opposed to walking. The advantages of this technique in interviewing are tremendous. As we have previously discussed interviewers spin questions unpredictably. The key is to put enough verbal "stepping-stones" into place. The good news is slight detours from planned responses work well. Also if a question is more of a departure than expected, this approach allows the flexibility to make the final jump to Side B, the end of the interview. For example, you could choose a combination of 1, 3, and 5 or 1, 2, 3, 5 and 6.

Remember "by hook or by crook" you have to convey your foundational information. In using the stepping-stone method, you are only memorizing small word groups or catch phrases that contain the information you want to convey. In jumping from one to the next you blend what you are saying like a normal, spontaneous conversation. It avoids the stiffness or contrived sound of a script. You will be perceived as incredibly articulate and thoughtful, both great qualities to convey to an interviewer. Here are examples of how each system works with real admissions committee questions. I am going to list 11 facts from my Inventory Checklist (some true, others not).

- Served 4-1/2 years in the Navy
  - Worked 60 hr/wk and took classes
  - Traveled tons →Saw wealthy places and very poor places →Am grateful
- Became a patient after a serious auto accident

○   Received kindness and compassion from family, friends and hospital staff
○   Learned about U.S. health care system firsthand
■ Volunteer in childhood illiteracy prevention program
○   Enjoy giving back
○   Serves as my "compassion" outlet
○   Learn more from students than I teach
■ Worked in hospitals

In an actual interview these would respond to questions in the Personal Values category. The first example is a "bridge" response, the second, a "stepping-stone" response. Again, these responses are from the Inventory Checklist.

Name three adjectives that best describe you.
Bridge Response:
"Three adjectives that describe me are: hard-working, compassionate and confident. I discovered these things about myself when I was working in a challenging environment at the hospital, as well as during my travels in the Navy. I also volunteer helping children learn how to read, which is a great way for me to give back and express my compassionate nature."

Stepping-Stone Response:
"The Number 1 adjective that describes me would have to be hard-working. After my service in the Navy I worked in hospitals while going through college. The next would be confident. I feel very comfortable with my abilities and myself as a person. Life experience and a good deal of travel have contributed to my self-confidence. Last I'd say, compassionate. After my auto accident I spent two

weeks in the hospital and was the benefactor of many people's compassion. It felt great and was very helpful in my recovery. I wanted to help others by showing them compassion and found the perfect spot at an illiteracy prevention program for children. It's been a fantastic experience."

Not bad – both contain good material. Both show a level of experience and preparedness. Each answer would probably fly, but what about a different personal values question?

What do you think about euthanasia?
Bridge Response:
"Uh, uh, I think that three things that describe me are being: hard-working, compassionate and confident. Why are you looking at me like that?"

Stepping-Stone Response:
"This is a tough issue for many people. Personally I don't support euthanasia. I guess it's because I've been the recipient of amazing compassion after my accident and have been able to give compassion through my volunteering efforts. These experiences have shown me that each one of us is a person who wants to live a long and meaningful life. Also, I observed many cultures as I traveled with the Navy. They dealt with their elderly and sick members in compassionate and productive ways. I feel more comfortable adopting some of those philosophies."

Let's try one more.

Name any person (living or dead) you would invite to dinner and why?

Bridge Response:
"Um, well, you see, I'd rather answer a question about words that describe me, because that's what I am prepared to say. Wait, why are you laughing? Okay, I would invite me to dinner because I'm hard working, compassionate and confident. Why do you keep laughing?"

Stepping-Stone Response:
"Wow, that's a tough one. I'd have to say I'd invite Mother Theresa, because she possessed an amazing combination of values that are important to me. She was so hard working and compassionate. I heard she frequently stayed up for more than 30 hours at a time caring for homeless people in her facilities. I just think it would be amazing to sit down and talk with her about what motivated her to demonstrate such compassion and how she could be so bold and confident as she went into foreign, impoverished cities to set up care facilities."

I hope the point is clear that the Bridge method works great if you know the exact question. The problem is if you get any other question, you must quickly improvise or you're toast. The Stepping-Stone method offers more flexibility so you can intelligibly address almost any question by using the categories and phrases you have prepared.

Preparing for the Interview Questions
After much ado, this is section is devoted to preparing the responses you will use during the interview. This compo-

nent requires a bit of work but it is critical for your success. The flow of information goes like this: inventory checklist → foundational information (Big 3 + "Is this person one of us?") → categories.

Here is what to do. First, gather all the foundational information you prepared in Chapter 4. Second, gather the remaining information from the Inventory Checklist. Prepare responses to possible questions for each of the above categories (or the categories you have created). In other words, for each of the above categories you are going to develop word groups to address the Big 3 questions and the question of "Is this person one of us?"

Please read Chapter 7 before addressing the category An Overview of You as a Person and an Applicant. This will be explained in detail later in the book.

Once all the responses are prepared, practice them over and over again. Using the list from the back of the book, ask yourself questions and answer them standing in front of the mirror. Watch your facial expressions and hand movements. Notice the rough spots, places in which you struggle to communicate. Look for places in which you do not appear to believe what you are saying.

Have family and friends ask you questions in an interview fashion. Ask them for feedback. Were you believable? Did you seem natural and comfortable? Did you fidget or bite your lip when you were talking? Videotape a mock interview or question and answer session. Play the videotape and grade yourself. Would you let yourself into medical school based on this interview? Did you look like you were relaxed and having fun? If not, try it again.

Many schools have career centers that provide help with job interview preparation. If your school offers this service, use it. The sessions are usually conducted with someone who specializes in interviews (not necessarily medical school interviews). The specific area the interview covers does not matter, because you are there for the experience. This will provide great practice in answering unexpected questions.

Tales from the Trail

I was horrible at interviewing when I started and my committee letter writers suggested I go over to the career center and do some video practice. I was so bad that I had to do the video session twice just to get to a place where I could even start to refine my skills. The video sessions were painful but very beneficial.

The next chapter contains detailed explanations of several questions you are likely to encounter.

Chapter 7
High Yield Questions

"I've heard that one before."

Let's consider the philosophy behind answering certain "high yield" questions. On almost every interview I was asked one or several of the following questions. (You can bank on seeing at least one of these or close replicas.) Many students blow these questions, usually because they do not understand the purpose of the question or how to properly address the issues at hand.

"Tell me a little about yourself."

This appears to be a simple question. Actually it is a trick question and the thing that makes it even trickier is that it comes right off the bat. It's an "ice breaker" question and is usually the first one asked. You may not even make it into the interview room before someone asks this question. Be ready or it will trip you up. This is the epitome of open-ended questions, but it is *not* the place for the story of your life. It's specifically designed to see where you will take it. This may be one of the reasons applicants struggle with it.

I can remember how open and undirected I felt when this question was asked. What's worse, I knew it was easy and that I was screwing it up! The key is to realize it's designed to give you the control. This may be a foreign concept but you have more control during an interview than you realize, especially with this question. Again, it's going to come at the very beginning of the interview. Since you know it is likely to be the first one out of the gate and can be "taken" which ever way you see fit, use it to outline the remainder of the interview. Condense all of your foundational information responses into very broad but interesting headings (like in an outline). Here's an example:

- I'm 25.
- I am a native of Salt Lake.
- I'm a person who is rich in life experiences, including 4 1/2 years in the Navy. I really value my experiences because they've played a large role in making me who I am.
- I think of myself as a well-rounded person.
- I have a strong love of academics and my work.
- I like to play hard: scuba diving, skiing, running.
- Family/social time is important to me.
- I have a strong relationship with the Lord.
- I am a person of influence.
- I have a passion for life.

Many other sources say, "Let the interviewer be in control of the interview". It is good advice, just a little too simple. A more realistic approach is to appropriately guide the interview as much as possible. This is done through your responses to the interviewer's questions. This is crucial, because the candidate (you) must convey x amount of information during that interview ("by hook or by crook..."). How in the world does anyone pull it off? The answer lies in, "Tell me a little bit about yourself." By giving the answer in the form of a brief outline of everything you want to convey during the interview, you present the interviewer with a tray of delicious hors d'oeuvres. The interviewer can pick any one of them and start asking you questions specific to that topic. For example, many people were scuba divers and wanted to know where I had dove, especially being in the Navy. Sometimes they wanted to ask about my skiing or specific military experiences.

Such things as a passion for sailing or bicycling are perfect entry points to address the Big 3 and "Is this person one of us." Of course an interviewer may chose items not on the hors d'oeuvres tray. But, by presenting interesting, bite-sized word groups, you can control the focus of the interview without appearing to do so. Here is a dialogue to show how it works.

Interviewer: "Tell me a little bit about yourself."

Candidate: "Well, I'm 25 and a native of Salt Lake. Having served in the Navy for 4-1/2 years, I'm a person who is well-traveled and loaded with life experiences. I really value these experiences because they have left me well-rounded. I love to study and work hard. It just comes naturally. I'm able to keep things in perspective and balanced by running and skiing with some scuba diving thrown in periodically. Family and social time are very important to me. They are such a stabilizing force for me."

Interviewer: "That sounds interesting. You mentioned strong family ties. Do you have family in the area?

Keep a running checklist in your head of what the interview has covered and what it has not covered. "OK, he asked about family ties and I used that opportunity to cover part of the Big 3 #1 and #2. With my next open-ended question I'm going to try and finish covering Big 3 #2." You get the idea.

"Why do you want to be a doctor?"
You likely have already faced this question from friends and relatives once you have said you want to go to medical school. I'm pretty sure I was asked this question in every interview. It's a lot like, "Tell me about yourself", and the same approach will work for both questions. A ton of students completely mess up this simple, potentially beneficial question. The outline form will work; just make it a little more focused. No need to repeat anything you just said. Focus more on addressing the "Is this applicant one of us?" question and Big 3 #1. Be sure to include some other key points, namely, I'm kind enough and smart enough to be a great physician. Most applicants feel comfortable going on and on about their kindness, compassion and patience, however, they stop short of conveying their intellectual prowess. This may sound crazy but it is one of the most common mistakes applicants make. They somehow don't think they should say something like they are smart enough.

Most of us learn as children not to brag and this is sensible advice. However, the concept of cognitive ability is not a bragging point; it's essential to being a good physician. Interviewers need to know you think you're smart enough to do this thing. Think about it. If I'm in the ER and my heart stops beating I don't want you to hold my hand and comfort me as I drift off to a permanent dirt nap. I want you to go get the Atropine and Epinephrine, know the dose and give me the drug to restart my heart. *After* you have been smart enough to recognize my grave medical condition, treat it and revive me, then hold my hand and comfort me. This is really important! Don't be afraid to tell them you are smart enough to be a great doctor. Here is an example of something to say:

> "In a nut shell, I think being a physician is the best fit for my personality and my skill set. I love to be around people and help them to feel better. Compassion seems to come naturally for me. [Maybe include a short story from your travels or previous work experiences.] I also think that I have the cognitive ability to thrive in the field of medicine. I love the mental challenges of biological sciences. I believe my GPA and MCAT scores bear this out."

"What would you do if you couldn't be a doc?
This is a very frequently asked question. I'm not sure I fully understand what interviewers are getting at with this question, but I think they're looking for a couple of things. They're trying to figure out if you have interests outside of medicine, but interests beyond just hobbies. So you wouldn't say, "Well, if I couldn't be a doctor I would focus on my inline skating passion." They're also trying to determine what drives you, what your motives are. It's kind of a clever way to address the issue because your drives shouldn't change just because your career does.

This is how to approach the question:

- Express remorse over the possibility of not being able to practice medicine (assuring them you are serious about this career).
- Cover some of your main values/strengths that would make you a good doctor.
- Put the answer in a context that reveals another aspect of you (an "other than" medicine interest).

This is how it might sound:

> "Wow, I would be pretty sad to not be able to practice medicine because I think it's the best profession for my talents and personality. However, if I couldn't be a doctor I would likely go into real estate [They would usually laugh at this point.] I love the mental challenge of crunching numbers and evaluating potential projects. This profession would satisfy my analytical nature. Unfortunately, it would not meet my needs for compassion and meaningful human contact. For that I would have to get involved in some type of community service project, maybe some type of mentorship program or homeless outreach."

This answer will leave most interviewers smiling and satisfied because they see what motivates you.

What will you do if you do not get into medical school?
This question has one focus: commitment. The interviewer wants to know how much you're willing to give to be a doctor. This is the perfect place to take the weaker parts of your application and put a positive spin on them (explained below).

This is a hypothetical question so don't be afraid to put out some bold hypothetical answers. Note: don't go overboard because you may be interviewing with that same person next year and they may ask you how your bold plans went, so keep your ideas within the realm of possible. Let's quickly cover the topic of the number of times you would reapply to medical school. I think there's a bit of game playing here, so be aware.

During the interview you should convey your intention to reapply as many times as it takes to get into medical school, period. Becoming a doctor is your passion and life's dream. Therefore, you will keep going until you realize that dream. Remember, this is a hypothetical question. You can't know exactly what you will choose in the future. Since you're speculating, do so in your favor. The number of times you are willing to apply carries serious weight in the admissions committee's evaluation of your application. It is a number that objectively demonstrates a commitment to becoming a physician.

Tales from the Trail

One woman I knew applied to the same medical school for five years. She was finally accepted on her fifth try. She became class president and is a wonderful doctor. Never give up!

Here is an approach to the question of what you will do if you are not accepted into medical school:

- Learn what the admissions committee thought was weak about your application and improve it. (Some schools will tell you what they thought was weak about your application or why they didn't accept you.)
- Tell them you will **reapply.**

- If, for example, there is not much research experience on your application, start working with a mentor on a research project about which you are excited.
- Work on improving GPA, MCAT scores, or other academic pursuits.

Here is how this strategy would sound as an answer:

"I think the first thing would be to find out what the admissions committee thought were the weaknesses in my application and address those specifically. I would then reapply. I would also start some research work with my mentor. Research is always something I've been interested in but haven't had the time to explore. Finally, I would enroll in some graduate science classes to further my learning and demonstrate my cognitive ability."

Ethical Questions

Be encouraged that you are much less likely to get this type of question during your residency interviews. However, on medical school interviews you are almost certain to face one of these types of questions. One thing that makes facing these challenging questions easier is to understand the 'what' doesn't really matter as much as the 'why'. That is to say your belief (the what) is subordinate to the reason behind it (the why). This is important because many applicants think they have to tell interviewers what they want to hear, or they believe there is one correct answer to a complex ethical question. These interviewers realize life is full of complicated, hard (sometimes unanswerable) questions. So, they're not looking for a correct answer; they're looking for the rationale behind the answer. They're likely interested in your thought process. They'd like to know whether you're realistic. Please, spend the time clarifying in your own head why you believe what you believe.

Common issues are:

- Abortion
- Stem cell research
- Cloning
- Euthanasia
- Suicide

Even taking into consideration everything we've covered, ethical questions can still pose difficulty for applicants. It is taxing to address and prepare for them. Here is a suggestion: read some articles in the lay press about each of these topics. Please don't read articles from a tabloid, rather those from respected sources that present both sides of the argument. Become familiar with the salient issues and spend time identifying your stance and beliefs on the topic, as well as why you hold those beliefs. Try talking to other people about these topics and share your beliefs with them. See how the conversation goes. Notice if they bring up weaknesses or areas of confusion in your explanation. Spend the time getting comfortable talking about these topics. If you do all of this, you will be very prepared for any ethical dilemma they present.

The concept of contradictions is an important one to bring up in this section. Interviewers are always trying to ensure you really believe what you say. They do not want to feel you're just telling them what they want to hear. The area of ethical questions is a common pitfall for applicants. Perhaps this is partly due to the fact that applicants don't realize they can have their own opinions, as long as they are reasonable and justified. This is an area of vulnerability in that the subject matter is of a sensitive nature. You're talking about abortion and suicide (areas in which you may have strong feelings) with someone you met only 10 minutes ago. It makes for an interesting situation. Here is how interviewers test applicants. Oftentimes, two questions addressing the exact same issue will be asked in two very different ways during the same interview. These types of questions can even be back-to-back! It is a low blow, but not outside the realm of everyday occurrence. The interviewer will see if you answer both questions with the same general philosophy. Just be watchful for ethical types of questions and always be consistent.

Interviewers often like to spin ethical questions in the context of current events. For example, during the Terry Schiavo incident, I can almost guarantee many a student was asked to give an opinion on the subject. To ensure you are prepared for current events, keep updated with one or more well-respected periodicals. Glance over the topics in each issue and focus on those that are medically related. Even if an interviewer does not address a specific current event, you can use recent medical news in some answers. Interviewers will perceive you as interested and informed.

Tales from the Trail

Stem cell research is a topic current medical school candidates should consider and read about. An interviewer can kill two birds with one stone with this issue; namely, see if you understand the science, as well as address an ethical issue. Often students blow this question based on lack of scientific understanding. Without this background, their ethical responses are incorrect or irrelevant. Don't be in this group of students.

"Is there anything that you wanted to share that we haven't addressed so far?"

Heck yes there is. This is a very important question and most interviews end this way. This and questions like it are designed to give you the opportunity to add anything you haven't had an opportunity to ask or share during the course of the interview. It is that important, last chance to complete the list of things that need to be conveyed during the interview. For example, if you haven't passed the second of the Big 3, or if you don't feel you've sufficiently addressed the question "Is this person one of us?", now is the perfect opportunity to do so. Here's an example of how this would go:

> "I didn't get a chance to tell you about my teaching experience, which I've really enjoyed. I worked as a TA for a physiology class as an undergrad. I found the experience to be amazing. I couldn't believe it but I found that I was learning more from the students than I was teaching them. I enjoyed sharing my knowledge and those 'ah ha' moments. I improved my own understanding on the subject. It also taught me communication skills and patience. These are two things I believe are important for all doctors to possess and I feel much more adept and comfortable with these skills after my work as a TA."

Even if you have covered all of your information, which happens, it is still important to use this opportunity to sell yourself. Create a summary statement, similar to your "tell me about yourself" response, but more focused on salient skills, values and characteristics. Remember, this often is your last chance to present information about yourself. It's imperative to use it wisely and seal the deal.

Note: this question may be presented as, "Is there anything that you wanted to share with the committee that you haven't had a chance to as of yet?", or it may be presented as, "There is one more spot left in the class and you are one of two people that we have to choose from, why should we pick you over this other person?" These two questions are getting at the same idea. The latter is slightly more suitable to a big picture summary, but both allow you to recap salient points and add any that have not yet come up. Again, this is really an important part of the interview.

"Do you have any questions for me?"

You bet you do. You will always have a question for them. I think this often is undervalued but it is very important. It also can be a little tricky because you want a good question that reflects your knowledge of the school but not one that brings up a sensitive topic and will offend the interviewer. This is absolutely not the time to ask about compensation. You also don't want to ask something that can be found on their website or in the information they send you. It makes you look like you didn't do your homework or prepare. Here are a few topics that you can use as ideas to help create your own questions:

- Have there been any big changes in managed care in the area or within the University?
- Are there going to be any changes to the curriculum?
- If so, when and what is the goal?
- If the curriculum has recently been changed, how is it going?
- What are the student responses to the changes so far?
- Are there any plans for changes of key faculty, such as upcoming retirements or promotions?

- Have any areas recently changed or are slated to change? (Ask only if they are not sensitive topics – see below.)

The topic of sensitive questions is a simple yet important one. Say a school to which you are applying has been reprimanded by the LCME (the organization that licenses medical schools) and told to fix certain deficiencies or they would be suspended. This is a very big deal and a bit of a sore subject for the school. In my opinion, it would not be wise to ask about this during the interview. It's a negative subject and likely to arouse a displeasing response from the interviewer. However, just because it's not a "question" topic, doesn't mean it's not an important area that you need answered. It is simply not a good idea to get those kinds of questions answered during the itnerview. You do not want to potentially put your interviewer in a negative frame of mind. They are your soon to be evaluator and advocate before the admissions committee. Keep it positive.

This is the way I approached this issue. At one school I interviewed, I found out the University and/or the associated hospitals had been bought by some big HMO type company. I asked how this new change would affect the medical school and what the interviewer thought of the situation. It worked great.

Big Picture: this is not a place to badger the interviewer about specific questions on course work, how the food in the cafeteria tastes or things of that nature. It is the time to ask one, maybe two, smart questions to show you are engaged in the interview process and have done your homework regarding the school.

Tales from the Trail

Many schools will have programs in which candidates may stay as guests in medical students' homes. Hosts drive their guests to their schools or campuses and show them where interviews are held. Take advantage of this program if it is available because: 1) it definitely helps to have someone show you where you need to go; and 2) it is an opportunity to ask students about current issues that are "appropriate" material for questions during the interview. This last point has the added benefit of exposing you to topics other than the ones in the brochures. The interviewer will perceive you as well-informed about the school.

CHAPTER 8
A DRY RUN

Secrets, Philosophy, Mechanics and Pearls

By this point in the book you have created your foundational information, as well as the categories you will use to easily answer most questions. However, you may be wondering how an actual interview day plays out. This chapter provides an overview of a typical interview day. It explains why certain aspects of the process exist, as well as giving some practical suggestions to help successfully navigate the process. Please keep in mind that each school's process is unique and your particular experience may vary. Nevertheless, this should give you the means to be adequately prepared. There is also some helpful information that is not in the other chapters.

Secrets of the Interview

This section provides some important information that most applicants do not know about and greatly limits their ability to succeed during the interview.

■ <u>Blinded by the light</u>

It is important to know some interviewers have read your file and some have **not**. It is very common if you have two interviews at a school that one of the interviewers will have read your application and the other will go in "blind." This is intentional. It prevents interviewers from being swayed by really good or really bad scores in your application. For example, if you have a 4.0 GPA, 39 on you MCAT and are published to the gills, an interviewer may focus too much on those outstanding academic accomplishments. He could overlook the fact you act like an arrogant jerk during the interview. Whereas, the interviewer who goes in "blind" would not know about your great scores and would just see the arrogance.

This "blinding" aspect plays a significant role in how you approach the interview. Remember, the rule is "by hook or by crook…" get a certain amount of information across during the interview. Understanding this, go into each interview assuming every interviewer is "blind." This will give you the proper mindset. It usually won't take too long to figure out if the person has or has not read the application. Sometimes it is okay to ask outright if a particular interviewer has read your application. Be careful not to imply the interviewer has been lazy or is unprepared. It would be acceptable to say something like, "I don't want to bore you by repeating what's in my application" and see what kind of response you get. However, don't worry if you are unable to figure out whether or not an interviewer has read your application. The safe bet is always to assume he or she has not, and cover all of the necessary information.

■ <u>Whose side are you on?</u>

Without overstressing the point, don't underestimate what's happening during an interview. Remember, schools offer more interviews than there are seats available in the upcoming class. This means tough decisions have to be made as to who will be invited to join the next class and who will not. You've made the cut on paper and been invited to interview, but that's not enough to get into medical school. The interview is the last and probably the most difficult in a series of steps to get into medical school.

In a recent conversation, a current member of the admissions committee at a large public medical school provided some very insightful "behind the scenes" information about the selection process. The take-home message was that the admissions committee is your adversary but your interviewer is not. Meaning, the committee is looking to "poke holes" in an application. If there's doubt about an applicant's potential, it is safer to not accept them. The thought is to let the candidate "mature" for another year and improve their application. However, the interviewer is truly your advocate before the committee and will try to present you in the best light possible. This does not mean the interviewer will automatically speak highly of you. No interviewer will cover up negatives or exaggerate positives. If the person does not believe you are a good candidate, he/she will say so. If you have convinced the interviewer you will succeed in medical school, he will actively combat the faultfinding of other admissions committee members who haven't had the benefit of meeting you. It would be impossible to overemphasize how important this concept is for your success.

The committee member shared another important insight. He said he found applicants do not like some of the tough questions he asks. They attempt to skirt the issues or give pat answers that do not really address issues. However, he doesn't understand applicants' aversion to the tough questions. He went on to say that, by providing applicants opportunities to answer challenging questions, he would have good material to present to the admissions committee and to use in their defense.

As these insights demonstrate, it is a disservice to you if interviewers ask only easy, non-substantial questions. An interview without depth weakens your case. It adds little to your application or to your chances of gaining acceptance into medical school. A smarter view is this: the admissions committee is trying to disqualify you. They will succeed unless you fully convince the interviewer (your advocate) you will be a fine addition to this medical school. Your job is to provide the interviewer with substantial evidence so he/she can go to your defense and change your fate. Some will claim this is an extreme view, but it is far better to over-prepare, than to under-prepare.

■ The questions behind the questions

Having a healthy understanding of the "weed out" nature of an interview can help you understand the dual nature of the questions interviewers ask. It's important to realize the actual question is often a "front" for something more important. It is of the utmost importance to figure out what the question and the interviewer are really after. Which one of the Big 3 questions or "Is this applicant one of us?" question is the interviewer addressing? You need to figure out what they're "getting at." This can be easy or difficult to see, depending on the situation.

For example, the question, "If I was the chairman of the Chamber of Commerce and you were a new doctor in town, why should I recommend you?" has nothing to do with promoting your future business as a doctor. It does, however, have everything to do with your attributes, values and skills as a physician. If you approach the question in any other way than explaining why you are the best doctor on the planet, you've missed the boat. Some applicants will respond by describing how convenient their office will be to other businesses and how they will have plenty of staff members to better serve the patients. They may add as an afterthought, "Oh by the way, I'll take good care of the patients." Wrong. Interviewers are not interested in your business plan. They are interested in whether you are a good person, smart and thorough. They want to know you love keeping up with current medical developments. They want to be assured you are going to do everything in your power to figure out what's going on with patients (make astute diagnoses), treat patients and help them to feel better.

Philosophy and Mechanics of the Interview

Let's quickly walk through the high points of a typical interview day. We will cover the important mechanics and mindsets that position you for success.

■ Scouting the site

A medical school candidate will usually travel all over the country to interview at various schools. It can be taxing on the emotions and on the pocketbook. Stress is the plate de jour, every jour. Figure out where you are supposed to be well before each interview day. If possible, go to the school the day before the interview. It is helpful and can ease your mind about some of the logistical problems you will encounter. If not, make sure you have good directions and feel comfortable using them. Allow plenty of time. It's better to sit and wait than to fret and worry about being late to the interview. This just isn't the time to practice your "cut it close" timing. When you get to the school, it is best to have time to relax, focus your thoughts and get in the interviewing zone. Oh yeah, I said, "interviewing zone."

■ Dress code

Let's briefly touch on dress code. The interview is not the time to push the fashion envelope. You may not like blue or black suits but I recommend you wear one. Whether it is subliminal, fair or unfair, dress is part of how you present yourself. Keep an eye on candidates who do not dress according to the prescribed norm. With rare exception, they do not give the impression of being strong applicants. They appear to be trying to differentiate themselves along the wrong lines.

Do you feel wearing a boring navy-blue suit would hamper you? It just isn't the real you? Think seriously about the expectations of interviewers and be really sure whether you're the one who wants to be remembered for an outfit. The few times I've seen this pulled off were by older applicants that had extensive experience in the business community and were very comfortable with themselves. If your favorite tie or handbag is bold or distinctive, that's fine. But stay within accepted norms.

■ In the waiting room

There is no escape from the applicant waiting room and it can be dead quiet. Once you're in the room it is fine to talk with other applicants. It will break the ice with people who would otherwise be a tense and unwelcoming group. No doubt this is due to the competitive nature of the process. The person sitting next to you is, in fact, vying for the same seat you want. However, you're not going to distinguish yourself by not speaking to fellow applicants. Just because you don't talk to the "enemy" doesn't mean you're the more competitive applicant. Does that make sense?

If you don't feel chatty, at least be cordial. The "silent treatment" can put anyone in a horrible frame of mind. Defensive, negative feelings are very damaging to carry into an interview. They limit your ability to flow and accomplish what you need to accomplish. You're not lessening your chances of getting into medical school by talking to fellow applicants. In fact, you may be improving your chances. At the risk of feeling a little dorky, start a conversation with the person next to you. Don't hunker down. Conversation with other applicants will help contribute to a proper mindset and a successful interview.

■ Timing

Most interview days begin with a small presentation about the school. Oftentimes they will spell out the schedule for the day, which may or may not include the length of time allotted for each interview. Knowing this data is very important. How you go about delivering all the necessary information will be markedly different between a 15 minute interview and a 45 minute interview. Remember, "by hook or by crook..." you have to convey a specific amount of information during the interview.

If the introduction did not include the scheduled length of time for each interview, feel free to ask. If you are unable to get an answer at that time, it is acceptable to ask your interviewer at the beginning of the session.

■ The interviewer arrives

Usually the interviewer will come to the waiting room and call your name. From the second they called my name and I laid eyes on my interviewer, I started gathering information about them. I would try to determine if he was tired, nice, happy, dressed well or shabbily, had distinctive jewelry on, new hair cut, nice shoes, anything. My observation didn't stop with my first glance. When I got into their office I would quickly scan the room for photos, diplomas and the Universities they came from, posters and anything that was clearly a personal touch and interest of the interviewer.

Tales from the Trail

I heard a story of an applicant that was taken into an office that wasn't his interviewer's. It was kind of funny as they commented on photos that didn't belong to the interviewer. He graciously told them his office was in another building. It turned out to be a good ice-breaker and a great interview.

Look for anything that will give you an angle on this person and, if at all possible, endear them to you. By evaluating the interviewer it is easier to know how to couch responses. Think of it this way, if you were asked to give a speech about science to a group of undergraduates and later speak on the same subject to Ph.D.'s, would the speeches be different? If you want to communicate your message, they better be different. Why then, would you deliver interview responses the same way each time? Each new interviewer is a new audience. Deliver your message to that audience. The point is communication.

From the moment the interviewer introduces themselves, appropriately guide the interview with your responses. It sounds a little much, but it's the truth. This is an important opportunity, so make the most of it. Of course you cannot come off as trying to control things, so take command in a subtle manner. As mentioned before, the hors d'oeuvre concept is a polite way to steer the conversation.

Present several topics as you answer questions. The topics will lead the interviewer to ask questions you are prepared to answer in a manner beneficial to your cause.

Confidence is another key to success and the following is an area where it can absolutely save you. There were several times that I felt like the content of my message wasn't as impressive as I would have liked. Nevertheless, I knew that most deficits in *what* I was saying could be made up for in the *way* I said it. I'm very serious about this. It's a lot like the ethical questions. It doesn't matter quite as much what I'm saying as long as I'm passionate and excited in the way I deliver my message. Please do not take this to an extreme. What you say does matter. However, keep in mind you can fill in many gaps and weak spots by means of the passion and confidence with which you deliver content.

So much of the interview is the impression you make. Do you have poise; are you confident; are you comfortable? The goal is to remain relevant and interesting, while presenting things in the context of a personal story.

■ Troubleshooting your application

During the interview I would try to bring up problem areas before the interviewer did. I view this like messing up as a kid. I found that I tended to get in less trouble if I went to my parents with the issue as opposed to them finding out about it on their own and coming to me. Please understand, I am not saying you air your dirty laundry but areas of your application that might be concerning or confusing should be addressed. An example might be a class you had to retake. It's not uncommon for people to struggle with Organic Chemistry and have to retake the course to prove they can do it. Let's assume your first year of Organic Chemistry yielded two C's. Not satisfied with your scores, you retook the course and got an A- and an A in respective semesters. I would approach the situation by preparing a concise explanation of any challenges, the corrective action taken and the lessons I learned. Here's how it might sound:

> "I remember how discouraged and frustrated I felt once I received my OChem grade. I just knew I could do better, and was determined to prove it. I spent some time looking back on problem areas and thought about how I could improve my understanding and my grade. I re-registered for the class, worked hard and performed at a level more in line with my abilities and my expectations."

This response addresses Big 3 questions #1 and #2, as well as "Is this applicant one of us?" Good medical students and doctors figure out what's going wrong and how best to fix it. They aren't afraid to learn from mistakes. They aren't afraid to work hard and redo something so that it can be done correctly. That's what this applicant has demonstrated. Does all this make sense?

Remember, many interviewers will not have read your file before the interview. If an interviewer reads your application after the interview and discovers a problem you haven't covered, it may create serious questions. Say you haven't explained the Organic Chemistry grade situation in the interview, the interviewer is left wondering, "What happened here?" "Why did they blow a whole year of organic chemistry?" "Did they just go retake the class with an easier teacher?" It leaves a good deal of room for conjecture.

Put yourself in the interviewers' shoes. You want to recruit the best candidates for your medical school. You run across something problematic in the application of someone you have interviewed. Would you want a firsthand explanation or would you rather be left to wonder? As we've said before, make the interviewer's (and the committee's) job as easy as possible. Don't leave unnecessary doubts in their minds. Explain anything that may produce doubt so as to alleviate the possibility of producing a potentially negative, doubting mindset in your evaluator.

■ Phrases you must avoid

I took a business fraud class when I was completing my MBA and I learned some very interesting facts about interviews. There are people out there called forensic accountants. Yes, I know, the term makes me laugh too. The role these people hold is to gather accounting type information that can be used in court, hence the term "forensic." These are the people who do audits in scandal situations like Enron, etc.

In the process of interviewing potential suspects they focus on certain key words and phrases that may indicate the person is lying. Some of those terms are "truthfully," "honestly," "to tell you the truth" and "in all honesty." It is an amazing phenomenon, but people will start to use these exact phrases when they are lying or trying to convince an interviewer of something about which they aren't fully convinced. The best advice is never, ever use these terms. Seasoned interviewers will be on the alert for this language. Interviewers who aren't aware of this phenomenon on a conscious level *are* aware of it on a subconscious level. Sentences beginning with, "To be perfectly honest," beg the question, "Well, was all the other information you told me a lie?" Weakening your image in this way is a disservice to you and your cause.

Most medical students probably aren't intending to lie in interviews. They just so want to get into medical school and so want to convince the interviewer of this desire, they succumb to the temptation to oversell. In turn, they say things that they don't fully believe. Now, even after that stern admonition, I must make a confession. Please read below.

Tales from the Trail

Despite the experience of conducting tons of interviews and even though I'd already written part of this book, I fell victim to the phrases, "honestly" and "to tell you the truth" in a residency interview. I wasn't lying, I was just unsure of my approach to the question. The interview was for a very competitive program, so I wanted to make a great impression. In attempting to pay the interviewer a complement on their program's web site, I spoke negatively about other programs' sites. My discomfort in speaking negatively about another program put me at a disadvantage. Feeling uneasy, I resorted to, "honestly" and "to tell you the truth". I don't think it affected me too much, because I realized what I had just said and didn't make the same mistakes again. I simply approached the issue in a different way and did it with confidence and poise.

■ Interview behavior norms

There are many fine resources that discuss in detail the prescribed norms of hand shaking, leg crossing and smiling. Instead of reinventing the wheel, here are some general ideas. Candidates already have several things on their minds and may not want to memorize etiquette books. It will serve you well to be genuine, comfortable and confident. This is a simple philosophy but it should keep you on the straight and narrow if you are ever unsure how to behave in a given situation. For example, a confident person usually has a firm handshake. It isn't a question of thinking about it. It is a question of doing it. Slumping posture, spread-eagle legs or wild gesturing are obviously to be avoided in any situation. Otherwise, whether you do or do not cross your legs ought to be up to you.

A genuine person usually has nothing to hide. If you are the smiling type, smile. If you do not ordinarily smile a lot, don't force it. Either is acceptable as long as it is a reflection of who you are. A fake, forced smile is worse than a genuine person who does not like to show the pearly whites. A confident and comfortable person usually has something to say and less of a propensity to say, "um, um" throughout the entire interview (a good thing *not* to do.) What follows is an example of how something might be good for one person but not another.

Certain interview books instruct candidates to avoid sitting on couches during interviews. A sofa can put you in a reclining position, making you appear "too casual." This recommendation is applicable for many people. It is difficult to sit on most couches and be comfortable while participating in an interview. One such book, however, also recommends against crossing your legs during an interview. I totally disagree with this comment. If I can't cross my legs during an interview I might as well leave. Crossing my legs is as natural as breathing. You, however, may feel the complete opposite way. Sitting on a couch may be very natural for you and facilitate communication, while crossing your legs may cause you to feel stuffy and unnatural.

In light of these inherent differences, the best recommendation is to **be** comfortable in your own skin and avoid extremes of behavior. Meaning, if you are a person who normally has a permanent frown on your face, you may want to get comfortable smiling occasionally during an interview. Likewise, if you feel most comfortable sitting cross-legged on the floor, find a new sitting position just for the interviews. (It is just not cool to pop a squat while wearing a navy-blue suit; sorry.)

Remember to answer sample interview questions while being videotaped. The stress of a video practice interview will likely expose nervous tics and inappropriate habits. Once you have identified these tics and habits, go through the video process again and make a conscious effort to avoid these behaviors.

Tales from the Trail

During my video interview sessions I continually stuck the tip of my tongue out of my mouth when I was thinking. It is the same kind of thing that kids do when they are concentrating or writing. When critiquing the session, my interviewer would advise me again and again to avoid doing this during an interview. It simply looks unprofessional. It took a conscious effort and a lot of practice to break this habit but I eventually was able to stop.

Pearls

Pearls are simple, high yield principles. We have covered all of these topics in previous chapters but this is a consolidation of many salient concepts. Spend time with these pearls. Let them sink in so this understanding is a part of you.

■ GENUINESS, AUTHENTICITY and ENTHUSIASM should ooze from you. The interviewer should leave the session thinking, "That was a really genuine person."

- **I AM DIFFERENT FROM THE PERSON NEXT TO ME.** Be looking for opportunities to let the interviewer know you have unique abilities, accomplishments, experiences and ideas.

- **POSITIVE ATTITUDE:** The interviewer has to remember you in a favorable light. The best way to accomplish this is to stay positive.

- **CARE FOR THE INTERVIEWER.** Do not think of the interviewer as an adversary, but as your advocate with the admissions committee. Make the interviewer's job easy. This is a healthy mindset.

- **IF YOU'RE NOT HAVING FUN, THEY'RE NOT HAVING FUN!** Yes, it is important to be having fun throughout the interview. It is a real time measure letting you know how the interview is going.

CHAPTER 9
A LIST OF QUESTIONS
AND CONCLUSION

"Are these things real?"

In order to help you prepare for your interview here are questions <u>used by actual admissions committees</u> and other preparatory committees, such as undergraduate health care careers committees. Some of these questions appeared in earlier chapters, some did not. Practice categorizing these and using them in your mirror and video practice sessions.

⇨ Tell me about yourself.
⇨ Why do you want to be a doctor?
⇨ What would you do if you could not be a doctor?
⇨ If you do not get into medical school, what will you do?
⇨ What are your strengths?
⇨ What are your weaknesses?
⇨ What are your MCAT scores?
⇨ What is your GPA?
⇨ Teach me something.
⇨ Tell me a joke.

⇨ What symbol/object describes you and why?

⇨ Who would you invite to dinner and why?

⇨ Is there anything I didn't ask you that you wanted me to ask?

⇨ Describe a challenging time or event in your life and how you got through it.

⇨ How are you a better candidate now as opposed to the last time you applied?

⇨ If I were the chair of the local Chamber of Commerce and you were a new doctor in town, why should I recommend you to my associates?

⇨ If you were placed in charge of all health care policy in the country, what would you change?

⇨ Give me three adjectives that best describe you.

⇨ What do you like to do in your free time?

⇨ What are some of your hobbies?

⇨ What do you think is the biggest problem facing medicine today?

⇨ What do you think health care will be like in 20 years?

⇨ If there was one seat left in the upcoming class and I had to choose between you and another applicant, why should I choose you?

⇨ What non-medical book are you reading?

⇨ What do you think a day in the life of a typical medical student is like?

⇨ Describe a time in your life when you had a leadership role and what you learned from the experience.

⇨ How do you plan to balance your family life and school?

⇨ What do you think makes a good leader?

⇨ What does the word "doctor" mean?

⇨ If you could stop the death of an entire village or your best friend, which would you choose and why?

⇨ Do you have local ties to the community?

⇨ What type of medicine do you want to practice when you finish your training?

A Note from the Author: I hope you have enjoyed reading this book as much as I have enjoyed writing it and sharing my passion for success in the interview. My intention is that this information helps you fulfill your dreams. Remember, nothing is as good a tutor as the interview itself. Take what you've learned here and modify it as you go along. It's about you. Use this information in conjunction with your own experiences and make it work best in your interviews. Good luck and godspeed.

To Order Copies of

THE MEDICAL SCHOOL INTERVIEW: SECRETS AND A SYSTEM FOR SUCCESS

by Jeremiah Fleenor, MD, MBA

I.S.B.N. 0-977955-90-7

**Order Online at:
www.shift4publishing.com**

**Order by Mail at:
P.O. Box 18916
Denver, CO 80218**

LaVergne, TN USA
22 January 2010
170873LV00002B/4/A